Dear American Christian

Dear American Christian

JESSE HAMILTON

RESOURCE *Publications* • Eugene, Oregon

DEAR AMERICAN CHRISTIAN

Resource Publications
An Imprint of Wipf and Stock Publishers
199 W. 8th Ave., Suite 3
Eugene, OR 97401

www.wipfandstock.com

PAPERBACK ISBN: 979-8-3852-3650-3
HARDCOVER ISBN: 979-8-3852-3651-0
EBOOK ISBN: 979-8-3852-3652-7

01/08/25

Contents

PART THREE. WHAT THE CHURCH IS *CONFUSED ABOUT*

Introduction

THIS IS NOW MY fourth book in practical theology.

The goal of each of these books has been the same, and it has been simple: to explore the gap between what we modern Christians *know* (or ought to know) and how we modern Christians *live*.

I am very thankful for the reception the first three books have gotten. Many have reached out with notes of appreciation and encouragement.

Unfortunately, however, a few have said that the books were not always easy to read.

I don't disagree.

The first, on prayer, was taken from a sermon I preached in 2003, right after I returned home from a very difficult first stay on the mission field. The second and third were written just after I left my PhD program in philosophy. All three, perhaps, were at times either too direct or too dense (or both) for the average reader.

I hope to correct these problems in this book.

At least the density part.

This little volume, in a very limited sense, is a simplified version of my second book, *Discipleship and the Evangelical Church: A Critical Assessment*, which looked at some of the ways the Evangelical church is failing to live out the vision of the New Testament.

I hoped to make that book robust enough for readers with a fair bit of theological knowledge. This book is much shorter and, I am sure, much easier to read.

However–this book is still somewhat direct in its language at times. Even though I try my best to take a balanced, loving, and measured tone, I do not believe it is helpful to put off direct statements entirely.

Most of the Evangelical church knows, I believe, where they have gotten away from the message and mission of Jesus. Some of our modern practices have gone on for generations. In the last hundred years or so in our culture, they have been called out by dozens of writers, from Bonhoeffer at the beginning of the 20th century, to A.W. Tozer, Jim Elliot, and Leonard Ravenhill in the mid-20th century, to many authors and pastors even today. My biggest influence in this regard has been my father, a pastor and missionary for over 40 years who has preached and prayed (along with my mother) for revival as much as anyone I have known.

Still–deep, abiding, and widespread change has been rare. It should be clear by now that certain problems in the Western church are perpetual. Direct and serious calls for repentance will always be needed.

But perhaps this has been true of the church in every age since the Spirit first fell at Pentecost.

I pray that this same Spirit attends you as you read this book. Only the power of the Spirit of God can help us fight free of the cultural blinders that keep so many of us in the West from truly following Jesus.

Jesus, son of David, have mercy upon us.
We need to regain our sight.

PART ONE

What the Church is *Missing*

I.

What's Going On?

Dear American Christian,

I have been a Christian for over 30 years. I grew up in a pastor's home in Louisiana. We were Baptists; we still are. I grew up on serious preaching, careful theology, and all-night prayer meetings.

When I was nearly 17, I became a true believer, a genuine follower of Jesus. My spiritual growth was slow in the beginning. I struggled with the usual things: doubt, spiritual laziness, immorality, discontentment, failure to love others.

Despite my youthful weaknesses, after college I followed my parents to the mission field. I eventually spent four years overseas, trying to reach college students with the gospel and working for my family's newly-formed NPO, which focused on disadvantaged women and children. By God's grace, a good bit of our work was blessed.

I came back to the States, got married, and then returned to the mission field for several more years, where the Lord continued to bless our ministry. Our only child, a daughter, was born there. Things were going well. Then, somewhat unexpectedly, the Lord brought us home.

Eventually, I felt called to go to graduate school, where I studied theology and philosophy. Then I wrote some books on the Christian life. I have now been married for over 20 years and have a 15-year-old daughter. We have been back in the States for over a decade, waiting on the Lord's guidance for our next missions opportunity.

I am very concerned.

Since we have returned, some crazy things have happened in our country. It seems our nation is falling apart.

Don't get me wrong; this kind of thing has happened before. Many times, in fact. Our nation once fought a civil war, for heaven's sake. It almost destroyed itself.

But this feels different, at least for my lifetime. Maybe it is, maybe it isn't. But it seems like our nation is rushing toward a giant cliff, a point of no return.

But there is something else, something I'm far more worried about.

I'm worried about the church.

Everyone can see that the church is having problems. I'm speaking mainly here of my own group, the Evangelical Protestants, but many of these concerns could be applied to the Christian church at large.

Local churches are dividing. People are unhappy. Many are leaving and going to other churches or denominations. Some are giving up the faith altogether.

Still worse, sin and apathy plague us. All of us–myself included, of course.

Perhaps you are one of the few who thinks the church is doing okay, especially compared to what is going on in society.

I would argue that you haven't been paying attention. This is also part of the problem.

The nation is getting worse.

The church is getting worse.

What are we Christians to do?

That is what this book is about.

II.

Three Areas of Concern

A LOT OF BOOKS have been written about how the church needs to change. Many of them have come out quite recently.

I'm very glad about this. But you may not be. You may feel that such books are discouraging. Perhaps some are.

Let me try to explain why I think another such book is needed. My reasons will be easy to understand. And although this book will not dive into these matters too deeply, my prayer is that what we do discuss will be enough to help us see the problem and decide to change.

My standard, of course, will be the Bible—the only source of authority for us Protestants. What Jesus taught, and what his apostles, inspired by the Holy Spirit and equipped with their own unique authority, taught.

First, I think the church today is *missing* some things. Some of these things are what Christianity is supposed to be all about—the essence of it, if you will.

Second, I think the church today is *distracted* by some things. These things are keeping Christians from doing what they are supposed to.

Third, I think the church today is *confused* about some things.

These categories are rather arbitrary, of course. But they will serve our purpose well.

The right way to think about all these things is clear in the Bible. Better yet, it is easy to understand.

The hard part is putting it into practice.

Let's start with what is missing in the church today.

III.

A False Gospel

THE FIRST THING THAT is missing in the church is about the gospel itself.

There is a wrong view of what the gospel is in Western culture today, and in many of our churches. This wrong view has been around for many years, but it has never been more widespread than today.

Especially in our own country.

I know this seems like a serious charge. And make no mistake, it is. Nevertheless, I think it is undeniable.

This wrong view goes like this: you can be a believer in Jesus, but you don't have to be a follower of Jesus.

You can be a true Christian, but not a disciple.

You can go to Heaven, but not actually live for Jesus on earth.

Nothing could be further from the truth.

Jesus made it clear that everyone has to be a disciple. Everyone has to follow him in obedience and submission. There is no other way to get to Heaven. But in our world today, and especially in our own country, this truth has all but disappeared.

I want to do two things now. First, I want to show you how Jesus preached this truth. I won't take long; I'll leave most of the Bible study for homework.

Second, I'll try to explain what it actually means to follow Jesus.

Keep reading, friend.

Your life may depend on it.

IV.

Whatever Happened to Repentance?

AROUND THE WORLD TODAY, but especially in America, the gospel often goes like this:

Just accept Jesus into your heart, and you will be saved.

Or, just believe that Jesus died on the cross for your sins, and you will go to Heaven.

Or, God loves you and has a wonderful plan for your life. Just receive it.

This is it, some preachers say; that's all you need to do.

You have probably heard some version of this.

I once walked into a Christian bookstore that was literally selling tickets to Heaven. Paper tickets—laminated, I was glad to see, for durability—that you could put into your wallet. The ticket said something like this:

"On the date listed below I accepted Jesus as my savior."

At the top, it said, "This ticket entitles the bearer to enter Heaven."

I am not even making this up. I wish I were.

I wondered what would happen if someone's wallet was stolen.

Of course, this an extreme and absurd example, but it represents the idea of the gospel we have today.

Just accept Jesus one time, whatever "accepting" means, and you are good to go.

There's only one problem with this.

This is not the way Jesus preached the gospel.

Don't get me wrong; believing in Jesus is an essential part of being a Christian. Jesus himself said this again and again. So did Paul.

What's more, we absolutely cannot be saved by our own good deeds. Only the life and death of Jesus will do, and we must receive this work of Jesus by faith. There are many passages in the Bible that say this.

But these are not the only verses in the Bible on the gospel.

A problem in our churches today is something we might call "selective theology." We zoom in on one verse, or one idea, perhaps even from one Bible author, and forget about the rest of the New Testament. We also ignore the fact that every verse, every chapter, and every book in the Bible has a distinct purpose, audience, and context, all of which impacts its content.

The Western church, especially in America, decided long ago that this distorted version of the gospel is the whole truth of the matter. But if we would truly be faithful to the Bible, we cannot pick and choose. We must carefully consider all the evidence. Pastors must preach through the entire Word of God, even the uncomfortable parts.

Jesus, for example, said the following:

"The time is fulfilled, and the kingdom of God is at hand; repent and believe in the gospel" (Mark 1:15). These are the first words Jesus spoke in the oldest gospel record, the book of Mark.

Notice something about this verse? There's an interesting word in there, right alongside the world "believe."

Repent.

It's a tough-sounding word; a hard word. It's also a command. And make no mistake: it's part of the gospel. You can't be saved without it.

Jesus made this clear. "Unless you repent, you will all likewise perish" he said later in the gospel of Luke (Luke 13:3).

When he sent his disciples on their first mission, it says they went out and "proclaimed as a herald" that men should repent (Mark 6:12). In the same story in Luke's version, it says they went out preaching the gospel (Luke 9:6).

Clearly, then, repentance is an essential part of the gospel.

Perhaps even the most foundational part.

Later in the book of Acts, the apostles preached again and again that everyone must repent. "Repent and return, so that your sins may be wiped away" Peter preached in Acts 3.

I trust the point is clear. If you don't repent, you will not have your sins forgiven; you will not go to heaven.

Again, this is not the gospel we often hear today.

So what does it mean to repent?

Glad you asked.

V.

What Repentance Is

To REPENT, QUITE SIMPLY, means to turn away from your sin. To stop doing it.

Many have argued over this word; some say it simply means a change of mind, while others say it means a change of life.

In the New Testament, it clearly involves both. It is a change of mind that results in a change of life.

"Bear fruit in keeping with repentance" John the Baptist preached in Matthew 3.

"Repent and turn to God, performing deeds appropriate to repentance" Paul preached in Acts 26.

You can't change your mind about something and not have it affect your behavior. That's the point here.

Repentance, then, above all, is a change of *heart*.

Let's pause and think about something.

Can you remember the last time you heard the word "repentance" or "repent" when someone was preaching the gospel? It's almost completely missing from our churches today.

I suppose the reason is not hard to guess. As I have said, "repent" is a hard word, a challenging word. Repentance causes pain and sorrow; repentance is serious.

I submit to you that we are not a serious people today. For the most part, we cannot do hard things.

More to the point, repentance causes us to confront our sin. And sin is not a popular topic today.

I once attended a Bible-believing megachurch where the pastor wouldn't even say the word "sin." He kept saying the word "mistake." It really was remarkable.

In the Bible, the word "sin" involves guilt; and guilt involves God's punishment. These are absolutely foundational biblical ideas.

Substituting words like "mistake" softens it.

You didn't mean to do it.

Hey, we all make mistakes.

You can see what's happening here.

This is the spirit of the age.

The sinful heart of man, when left to itself, will always move toward what is easy, and not toward what is hard. Toward comfort, not discomfort. Toward pleasure, and not pain. We will always soften the idea of sin when we become too comfortable with it.

And that's what's happened to the gospel today.

It is no longer about our sin and our need to repent. It is about making us happy.

It is no longer about God's holiness, or his wrath against sin. It is only about his love.

But that is not the gospel of the Bible.

VI.

What the Apostles Preached

ONE OF MY DAD'S seminary professors in the 1970s was on to this problem.

"After Jesus, who do you suppose were the best, most accurate, most powerful preachers of the gospel who ever lived?" he would ask his students.

Of course, the answer was always the same: the apostles in the book of Acts. They were the first preachers of the gospel after Jesus, and they were powerfully filled with the Holy Spirit.

"How do you think they preached the gospel?" he would ask. "Did they start by talking about God's love, or did they start with man's sin and God's wrath?"

"God's wrath?" the students guessed. They knew where this was going.

"Correct" said the professor. "There are many gospel sermons recorded in the book of Acts, preached by several of the apostles. And how many times do you think God's love is mentioned in the book of Acts?"

"10?" guessed the students.

"Fewer," said the professor.

"Five?" said the students, growing uneasy.

"Lower," said the professor.

"Two?" said the students, at this point a bit disturbed.

14

"The word "love" is not found in the Book of Acts even once" said the professor solemnly. "Not as a noun, a verb, an adjective, or an adverb."

His point was clear. Apparently, the apostles didn't think the gospel had to start with God's love.

Apparently they didn't feel they had to mention God's love at all.

Powerful stuff. But let's hold on a moment.

We know God's love is important; some New Testament writers, such as the Apostle John, mention it often.

But for Jesus, that's not where the gospel begins.

And just as our Lord began with repentance as he announced the arrival of the kingdom of Heaven, so did the apostle Paul. His famous gospel letter, the book of Romans, begins with the proclamation of . . .

The wrath of God, which is waiting to be poured out upon all sinful men, upon all who do not repent.

Go back and read it for yourself. Romans 1, verse 18.

He doesn't get to God's love until Chapter Five.

Do you think this is a problem in our day? That we are far too often only getting part of the story? I do.

I think it all goes back to our view of God.

VII.

Remaking God in our Own Image

IT HAS BEEN SAID many times, but it needs to be said again:

We human beings have a great tendency to recreate God in our own image.

The God of the Western church is largely a modern invention. So is the modern gospel. So, as we shall see, is the modern Christian life.

As we have said, as men continue in sin, they begin to soften toward it. Once this begins to happen, the difficult things disappear.

A God who is holy and hates sin, whose wrath is revealed against all unrighteousness, becomes a God who is always loving and accepting.

Which is what we have today.

Don't get me wrong; God is incredibly loving, merciful, and gracious. Like a loving father, he will accept any sinner who truly repents. This is beautifully illustrated in the famous parable of the prodigal son (Luke 15).

And when we become his true children, he bears with our weaknesses and failures better than any earthly father ever could. This is wonderfully described in Psalm 103.

The love, mercy, and compassion of God are truly beyond all understanding.

16

But that is not the only message we need to hear. In fact, as I have argued, it is not the first message we need to hear.

What has happened today is clear. In many cases, we have truly accumulated teachers according to our own desires (2 Timothy 4:3).

The great, awesome, fear-inspiring holiness of God, a central biblical truth, has all but disappeared. As we said, now God is only there to increase our joy.

The seriousness of sin has vanished. Now we focus only on forgiveness.

Calls to repent have ceased. Now, we merely accept the blessings of the gospel and go about our earthly lives.

In our peaceful slumber, we have drifted far from shore.

VIII.

The Call to Discipleship

WE COULD TALK ABOUT God's holiness and how essential it is for pages and pages. It really is incredible how this one missing element has impacted so many things in the modern church, from how the gospel is preached, to how we live our lives, to the kind of worship we now prefer, and so much else. Having a right view of God is foundational; without it, everything else goes askew.

Think about the call of Isaiah, for example; it wasn't until he saw God for who he really was, in all his holiness, that he realized his own sinfulness; that he viewed himself properly (Isaiah 6). And it was only then that God used him for ministry.

But for now, there is something else missing from the gospel today, and we must hasten to consider it.

It is the call to give up everything and follow Jesus.

When Jesus was on the earth, he called everyone to follow him and be his disciple. This is evident all throughout the gospel accounts.

In Luke 14, he puts it like this:

> Now large crowds were going along with Him; and He turned and said to them, "If anyone comes to Me, and does not hate his own father and mother and wife and children and brothers and sisters, yes, and even his own

life, he cannot be My disciple. Whoever does not carry
his own cross and come after Me cannot be My disciple."

And all along, he makes it clear: to fail to do so means losing
eternal life (Matthew 16:25–26).

It is absolutely clear in the teaching of Jesus: no one can come
to him for forgiveness, for eternal life, without following him as a
disciple. There is no difference between a believer and a follower.

Accepting Jesus means taking all of him. Not just his blessings, but his sufferings. Not just his forgiveness, but his mission.
His call. His teaching. His Lordship. His way.

His very life.

This is what following Jesus means; this is what being a disciple means.

It is incredible how the Christian church today has lost sight
of this.

Many assume that discipleship is something extra; something
added on after forgiveness.

This is not the way Jesus presented it.

Please, friend, return to the Bible. Pick it up and read it. See
how Jesus called all people to follow him in the gospel accounts.
See what he said about discipleship. See how serious it was.

You will see that for Jesus, discipleship was a straightforward
matter. It meant two simple things: becoming like him in his character and continuing his mission in the world.

They are really only one thing: imitating Jesus. This is what it
means to follow.

Following Jesus is neatly summarized in the two great com-
mandments: loving God and loving man.

Jesus loved his father with all his heart. He also loved people
with all his heart.

His heart beat for his father to be honored and glorified in the
world, and for lost people to come to know his father.

It beat for the holiness of God's people; for the purity of God's
message; for sinners to come to repentance; and for the poor, de-
spised, and broken to be loved and cared for.

These things were more important to him than food (John 4:34).

And he called all people to show the same level of intensity, the same level of commitment to these things. This is why he called on all men to follow him; and this is why he said that to follow him, we must "deny ourselves" and "take up our crosses" (Matthew 16:24).

As so many have said before, to follow Jesus means to die, that you might live.

It is a total abandonment of one's life, and an all-out commitment to the mission of Jesus.

Surrender and dedication. Absolute and final. Nothing held back.

Where is this message in the church today?

IX.

Giving Jesus Everything

I WANT TO TALK a bit more about discipleship, so that there is no confusion.

I'll start by saying it again: there is no difference between a believer and a disciple. You are either both or none. You either believe in *and* follow Jesus or you do neither.

When you come to him, you must take all of him. That is how Jesus presented it. You either submit to his teaching and Lordship, or you reject him entirely. There is no middle ground.

But what does this really look like today?

I have said that following Jesus involves two things: surrender and dedication.

What must you give up to follow Jesus, and what must you commit to?

In his own day, people actually gave up everything. Think about it: in order literally to follow Jesus around, they had to. And if they weren't willing, once again, Jesus said they couldn't be his disciples.

I believe that in a very real sense it requires nothing less today.

A follower of Jesus is someone who has given up everything and made the pursuit of Jesus and his mission his main purpose in life.

He may not literally be leaving behind family, friends, home, or other things, of course. But he is surrendering everything nonetheless.

Perhaps more than anything else, he surrenders all *ambition* to the will of Christ. His interests, his pursuits, his talents, his future plans, his career path; the follower of Jesus gives these up. He says to the Lord: "Thy will be done. Tell me what to do."

There is a very common myth in the Christian community today. It goes like this: "God wants me to use my natural talents for his glory. My purpose in life is to develop my abilities, in whatever area I am gifted in, and glorify God in that field."

This is not how Jesus presented it. This very popular idea is simply wrong.

The call of Christ is this: first, leave everything behind and follow me. Then, commit to serving me and my mission as your true priority.

Then, I will tell you what to do.

It may involve your natural abilities. It may not. Jesus says: I will decide.

In America today, few seem to have grasped this. The lure of success through the development of our talents and abilities has stolen our hearts. All is merely self-interest and self-promotion.

The call of Christ to discipleship cuts through all of this.

If anyone would come after Jesus, he must deny himself, take up his cross, and follow him (Matthew 16:24).

Friend, have you done this?

X.

The Heart of the Matter

OF COURSE, WE CANNOT know in advance what following Jesus will look like in every person's life.

In his day, as I have said, it was obvious. Following was literal. It meant leaving behind everything to live and travel with Jesus. To do what he said; to learn from him and imitate him.

Is it really possible to have the same level of surrender and dedication to Jesus today, now that he has gone to Heaven?

I have argued that in a very real sense it is. And I would argue that we must.

Remember, there is only one category of "Christian." You either follow Jesus or you don't.

It begins with the heart. Jesus said the greatest commandment was to *love* God, with all one's heart, soul, mind, and strength (Mark 12:30).

Do you love Jesus supremely? Look inside your heart. What are you living for? What gets you excited every day? What are your hopes and plans? What do you dream about?

If it is not the person of Jesus, the teaching of Jesus, the death and resurrection of Jesus, and the mission of Jesus—his church, the gospel, the lost and needy of the world—then perhaps we need to ask ourselves some tough questions.

It is actually rather easy to test ourselves on this. All one has to do is open the gospel accounts and read of Jesus. Read what he taught and preached. Read what he did. See how he prayed. Look at what he rejoiced over, and what he mourned over.

Does your emotional life match his? Does his teaching bring you joy and excitement? Do his actions draw adoration from your heart? Do you want to be with Jesus every moment, as a true follower? Do you want to hang on his every word? Do you want to do what he is asking you to do, with all your heart? Do you want to imitate him every day? Do you long to sacrifice yourself for his cause? Are you willing even to die for Jesus?

I am not saying we will feel this way all the time, of course. But if your life is not at least marked by these thoughts and feelings on a regular basis; if other things excite you, so much so that Jesus is an afterthought, or, at best, a weekend fancy, then perhaps you are not really following Jesus.

Of course, Jesus warned against the kind of love for him that falls short of obedience. He knew well that many would come to delight in him but be unwilling to truly follow him. Delight in Jesus, loving him from the heart, is foundational; but it doesn't end there.

Just as with repentance, true love for Jesus starts inside of us, but shows itself outside. And since the love that God calls us to is absolute—heart, soul, mind, and strength—there will be signs.

We will spend time consistently with Jesus in his Word and prayer–because we want to. We will talk about Jesus in our daily lives. We will help the poor and needy. We will be truly sad when people don't know him, and try to reach them. We will rejoice with righteousness and hate sin, and we will fight against it with all of our being.

We will not be living for ourselves. Our own desires and ambitions; money, success, and fame; these will be nothing to us. Our one thought, our one driving desire and ambition, will match his. Doing God's will and accomplishing his work will become our very food. All other delights, desires, and ambitions will fade away.

Jesus will become our everything.

It won't ever be perfect in this life; Jesus never expected that.
But it will be real. And over time, it will be growing.
More of him and his mission. Less of ourselves.
Is this the pattern in your life?
If not, do you long for it to be so?

XI.

The Missing Spirit

WE HAVE ARGUED THAT at least two things are missing from many presentations of the gospel today: repentance from sin and the call to follow Jesus in absolute surrender.

There are many other things that are missing in our churches. Truth—the serious study, preaching, and application of God's Word—has long since disappeared. There are very few churches where pastors actually preach through the entire New Testament and tackle all the passages it contains, including the difficult ones.

The result has been a shallow, superficial church. Which makes sense, because we live in a shallow, superficial age.

Americans don't think or read anymore, at least not anything worth reading. We can hardly even sit still.

Some have suggested that the answer is more theological education. We need to make our churches smarter, or at least more well-informed.

I disagree. Don't get me wrong; more serious study of the Word of God is essential, as I have just said. There is so much truth that God included in his Word that is being ignored, Sunday after Sunday. This is tragic.

Studying the Word of God is not necessarily the same as gaining more theological knowledge. There are so many theological systems today that are bloated, unnecessarily complex, and frankly unbiblical. Many are easily led astray into error by their love of theology.

But I believe there is something even more important that is missing.

It is not the Word of God; it is the Spirit of God.

I know; these two are inextricably linked. However, there is a very real danger that it seems many of us do not even realize is possible.

You cannot have the Spirit of God without the Word of God. When the Spirit comes, it teaches (John 14:26). When the Spirit fills a person, he speaks the Word of God in all boldness (Acts 4:31). When the Spirit is there, it wields the Word of God, the Sword of the Spirit, like a mighty weapon (Ephesians 6:17). You cannot have the Spirit without the Word.

But I believe you can have the Word without the Spirit.

And this may very well be the greatest of all problems in the Evangelical church today.

Think about it; we have the Word of God with us nearly all the time. It litters our bookshelves and collects dust on our end tables. It is splashed on our walls, our refrigerators, our coffee mugs. It is constantly on our radios, in our music, and in the words of our friends. It passes through our minds on a consistent basis every day.

In most Evangelical churches, even the weakest of them, we hear more truth on a Sunday morning than whole people groups have heard in a lifetime.

But what is our attitude toward it? Often, it is deadness and coldness. Apathy.

The problem with the church today is not that we don't *have* the truth. Most American Christians have read the Bible dozens of times over, and it is easily accessible to us.

It is not that we don't *know* the truth. Most of us know enough truth to teach a college-level Bible class.

The problem is that we often don't *feel* for the truth. We don't, in fact, love God with all our being, as we discussed in the previous chapter.

Only the Holy Spirit of God can help us do so.

The Holy Spirit is the one who *feels*.

The Holy Spirit takes the Word of God and ignites it into an all-consuming flame within our souls.

Again, we do have love; but we love other things. Our hearts are divided, distracted, and more often than not totally enamored with earthly things.

Things such as our own ambitions, which are almost always self-centered. Our own success. Our pleasures. Our entertainments. Our comforts. Even our work.

There are so, so many comforts and pleasures in our country. There has never been a more comfortable country than America. There are so many earthly distractions today, at the click of a button.

The result is that the great problem we all face is simple—we love our lives and this world too much.

As a result, the church of God is failing. It is failing in its most basic duty: to be salt and light in this needy world. As has been said before, the church has been conquered by the world; from within.

There is only one solution. Unsurprisingly, that solution is the one thing that is missing from the church more than any other thing.

Seeking God's face in desperate prayer, so that the Holy Spirit, with all his love and zeal for the things of Heaven, might return to us.

This is our only hope.

XII.

Getting Back to Prayer

ALL THROUGHOUT THE BIBLE, men and women of God are seen praying. Nowhere is this more prominent than in the Book of Acts, when the newly formed church gathered to pray. The Holy Spirit had fallen upon them; it continued to fill them. And they were marked by serious prayer.

Small wonder that the New Testament tells us repeatedly to "pray at all times."

The church today prays at no times.

I believe there are several reasons for this. Two I have mentioned already.

Prayer is hard, but we modern American Christians are soft. Prayer is spiritual work; but we are too busy indulging our flesh.

And prayer is a key sign of a heart in love with God. But we are in love with other things.

The man who prays does so because he wants the same things that God wants—in his life, in the church, and in the world. His cry is that of Jesus—thy kingdom come, thy will be done, on earth as it is in Heaven (Matthew 6:10).

Perhaps we often don't pray because deep down we really don't care.

Jesus wept over the perishing, but many of us couldn't care less about them. Jesus was moved to anger over the corruption of

God's church, but this doesn't bother us at all. God hates sin with an infinite hatred, but we've learned to tolerate and excuse it away.

It all starts from within.

How do we learn to care? Somewhat paradoxically, we need God's Spirit. And to get it, we must come to God and ask him for it.

People do pray when they know that only God can help them. It has often been said, and it is true; it is the truly desperate who pray.

It makes sense to say that we will not be desperate, we will not pray, until we *feel* desperate. And we will not feel desperate, perhaps, until we see our true need.

Sometimes I wonder: do we really know how much we need God on a daily basis?

Here, then, is a Bible truth we cannot pass over.

XIII.

Our Need for God

LET US CONSIDER A little theology. I am afraid we must.

It has long been the teaching of the church that no one can choose God on their own. God's grace must come first for anyone to be saved.

This was first affirmed by the church 1,500 years ago in the Council of Orange, when the views of a monk named Pelagius were condemned.

Today, as we all know, there is a wide-spread view that we have the kind of free will that allows us to choose God on our own, without his grace.

That we are fully in charge of our own salvation.

This view, for all intents and purposes, is heresy.

Yet it is safe to say that it is now the dominant view in the Evangelical church.

I include this little anecdote first of all to point out how far the church has drifted in our times.

I believe the Bible's teaching on this issue is clear. But there is another reason why I am including it here.

I believe that a failure to understand the absolute necessity of the power of God is one reason why the church has little power today, and little prayer.

You see, it is one thing to believe that we can choose God first in salvation; that we don't need God's help to come to him. I believe, along with virtually the entire church down through the ages, that this is clearly unbiblical, and a serious insult to God; but let's leave that for now.

It is quite a different thing to believe that we don't need God's help *after* salvation; his power to live the Christian life.

This is also heresy; and it is incredibly dangerous.

Consider this. It may sound odd based on what I have said here, but I believe it is entirely possible for a genuine Christian to believe that we can choose God first. I know many such people today.

I am not sure it is possible to be a Christian and believe you don't need God's help to live out the Christian life.

For one thing, it would imply that you are not seriously reading the Bible. Again and again, the New Testament affirms that we cannot do what God is calling us to do without his help, his Spirit.

Jesus told the disciples to watch and pray that they may not enter into temptation, because the spirit of a person may be willing to do the right thing, but the flesh is weak (Matthew 26:40–41).

Paul said that we can only put to death the deeds of our bodies, our flesh, by the power of the Spirit of God (Galatians 5:16). In this context, the flesh is the sinful you, the you without the Holy Spirit. Those in the flesh cannot please God (Romans 8:8), and the flesh and the Holy Spirit are set against each other (Galatians 5:17).

Only by walking in the Spirit can we please God; and we need his help, his Holy Spirit, to accomplish any spiritual good.

To read God's Word, or even to want to read it. To pray. To love and forgive. To resist temptation. To be unselfish; to care for others. To give expecting nothing in return.

None of this can happen without the grace of God–his Spirit.

This is why prayer is so important.

When we pray, we are asking for God's help, for ourselves and others.

When we pray, we are looking to the only source of power, deliverance, and spiritual good.

Prayer shows our dependence on God; its shows that we realize God is our only hope.

It also shows that we know we are in a spiritual battle.

XIV.

The Spiritual Battle

MOST CHRISTIANS DON'T REALIZE what is actually going on all around them.

There is a spiritual battle taking place between the forces of good and the forces of evil–just like in one of those fantasy novels that are so popular today.

Only this one is real. And deadly serious.

This battle can be seen all throughout the Gospels and the Book of Acts. As they sought to spread the gospel and reach others with God's love and truth, Jesus and his apostles were involved in constant struggles against the supernatural forces of evil.

The Bible presents the evil one as a real being, no matter how unreal he seems at times. His goal is simple: to bring dishonor to God by disrupting his purposes.

He will do this by bringing temptations to every kind of sin: anger, unloving speech and actions, immoral thoughts and feelings, selfishness, spiritual laziness, and so much else.

He is far wiser than we are, and his schemes are often subtle and hard to spot until it is too late.

I believe he has the American church right where he wants us.

He is watching and waiting, to be sure. But he doesn't do much at the moment because most professing Christians are not really in the fight.

After all, it takes two to tangle.

Christians are called in the New Testament to rise up and wage spiritual warfare; to overcome sin and temptation in our own lives and work hard to reach others with the love and light of Jesus. This is seen in the famous passage in Ephesians 6:10–20 and in many other places. But most of us are too bogged down in our own everyday lives to be of much spiritual use.

Let's just be honest about that.

Winning the spiritual fight every day is our goal. But most of us are stuck in sin patterns and simply not making real progress in our personal holiness. When we are avoiding sin, we aren't trying to pray or reach others. Mostly we are just enjoying life.

We Americans spend so much free time on ourselves. We are all guilty of it. There are so many ways to entertain ourselves these days; to pass the time in pleasurable ways. Not all of it is sinful, of course. But there is a battle going on. And we are to join it.

Those who are able to live holy lives, and who are actively thinking of others and trying to reach them, will most certainly feel the devil's attacks. They must stay the course and stay in the fight.

When you begin to make progress–when you begin to overcome sin and pray–there are three fronts, if you will, that the devil will try to attack: your personal life and holiness, including your relationship with your family; your relationships with your fellow Christians and the church; and your impact on the world of unbelievers.

The evil one hates your holiness; he wants you to sin. He wants you to sin so much that you doubt God and your own salvation. He wants you to so focus on your sin, or be stuck in it, that you are either too crippled by guilt to fight or simply too unconcerned about the things of God.

He also hates your happiness, including in your family relationships. How often he tries to sow discord between husbands and wives or parents and their children!

The evil one hates the church. As we have already mentioned, he wants churches to be watered down and to avoid the clear teaching and preaching of God's Word. But he also wants the people of God to be fragmented and fractured.

He has already done this successfully in so many ways throughout history; but in most Evangelical churches, he simply keeps people uninvolved in each other's lives. One of his greatest ploys, it seems, is to keep us apart, to keep us from growing closer and joining forces.

Because when the church comes together—there is strength in numbers. There is encouragement; there is mutual ministry; there is faith-building.

The evil one also hates when unbelievers hear the gospel. But above all, I believe, the evil one wants God's people to avoid praying, something the New Testament tells us to do "at all times" (Ephesians 6:18), as we have seen.

We are to pray, as a united people, for each other and for God's purposes in the world, because only God's power will do. Gathered, corporate prayer is *so* important in the purposes of God; it is so much more powerful than individual, scattered praying.

God delights to inhabit his gathered people, and he will most certainly be eager to hear their corporate prayers.

But God's people are too distracted to pray. And they can't come together and pray because church leadership has not presented a unified vision for prayer by standing on the truth.

It really is a tragic situation.

But it is not hopeless.

The infinitely powerful God of the universe is a mere repentant heart and sincere cry away from unleashing all the spiritual power our souls and the church need, to rise up and be the men and women of God we are called to be and to reach a lost and dying world for Jesus.

The only questions that remain are these:

Who will give themselves over to seeking the grace and power of almighty God in prayer?

And who will persevere in prayer until they see God work?

XV.

Cheap Grace Revisited

A FINAL THOUGHT BEFORE we move on.

There is a newfound emphasis on the gospel today.

I have heard "gospel-centered" preachers say something like this: The key to gaining assurance and growing in holiness is to focus more and more on the truth that Jesus died on the cross for our sins, paying our penalty and securing forgiveness with God.

Obviously there is some truth in such statements. So much of the New Testament is focused on the glorious reality of what Jesus did for us.

Once again, it is clear in the Word of God: our own righteousness, our own good works, could never atone for our sin and guilt. God provided his own righteousness, in the perfect life and death of Jesus, to appease his wrath. Jesus did what we could not do, and our duty is to put our faith wholly in what he has done (Romans 3:20–28), trusting in him alone for our salvation.

But as we have seen, this notion can so easily be abused.

When we consider the entire range of the New Testament evidence, as we have said, the gospel is never simply "believe in Jesus." Jesus demanded that everyone take *all* of him, including his teaching, his Lordship, and his mission. Coming to Jesus in faith involves repentance from sin and a heartfelt commitment to follow Jesus in absolute surrender. Jesus and his apostles never presented the gospel in any other way.

As we have noted, these elements are often missing in churches today. Presenting a different gospel than Jesus presented, however, is a false gospel.

In addition, in the New Testament, the reality of Jesus's life and death on our behalf actually strengthens our obligation to do good works.

It doesn't free us from pursuing them; it frees us from relying on them.

Thus, no Christian can use the truth that Christ died on the cross for their sins to excuse or avoid dealing with their remaining sin. But this is what seems to be happening today.

This is an incredibly important issue. Let me show you what I mean.

Paul presented faith in Jesus as the essential ingredient of salvation; but he also described salvation as being *joined* to Christ in his death to sin. Salvation is not merely accepting God's forgiveness in Christ; it is understanding that we are "united with Him in the likeness of his death," so that "we too might walk in newness of life" (Romans 6:4–5). It is recognizing that we are now "enslaved to God" (Romans 6:22), bound to obey him.

There is more.

Thankfully, many Christians understand that their good works cannot save them. But this is not the whole picture on good works.

Jesus made it clear in his teaching, again and again, that only those who bear fruit, who do good works, will enter the kingdom of Heaven. Go back through his teaching in the gospel accounts, beginning with the Sermon on the Mount. See what you find there.

In Romans 5–8, Paul makes the same point. Here, salvation is presented not as the mere acceptance of some facts about Jesus; it is presented as a process through which we are joined to Christ and begin a new life in the Spirit. This life in the Spirit produces good works, and it is through these good works that we will eventually gain eternal life. Romans 8:9–14 couldn't be any clearer—or more sobering.

This same truth is found in Galatians 6:7–9. Whatever you sow, Paul says, you will reap; and eternal life is only for those who "sow to the Spirit." Indeed, those who practice the deeds of the flesh will not inherit the kingdom of God (Galatians 5:21).

The writer of the Hebrews also affirms this idea with absolute clarity (Hebrews 12:14). In fact, in the space of one chapter, the author of Hebrews affirms both the way of salvation by faith in Christ, and the fact that those who continue in sin will not be saved (see Hebrews 10).

So much for the gospel of Paul being different from the gospel of Jesus, as some critics have claimed. They are actually in perfect agreement.

And yet–how can both of these truths be true? How can our good works not merit anything for us, and yet be something we cannot be saved without?

We must be careful here; but it really is a simple matter.

A key point to understand is that the Bible often talks of salvation as a process and a future event. It is not just that we "have been saved" (Romans 8:24); we "are being saved" (I Corinthians 2:15) and we "will be saved" (Romans 5:9). Our full and final salvation, biblically speaking, occurs when we are finally in Heaven and have passed the ultimate test, when we stand before God in the final judgement.

In addition, as the New Testament makes clear, God's purpose for us is not merely to *declare* us righteous at the beginning of this process; it is to *make* us righteous. It is a process, the whole of which is precious to God. And make no mistake: God *will* make his true people holy in this life.

So we can say it without apology: good works cannot save us, but we cannot be finally saved without them.

This is not a contradiction. But it is a missing note in most churches today.

I believe it desperately needs to be recovered.

Again, we must never affirm that our own deeds can make us right in the sight of God. Nothing can for sin atone, as the hymn says, except the blood of Jesus. The New Testament makes this clear again and again.

We hear about this all the time in pulpits today.

We so rarely hear the other part.

Bonhoeffer was right, so many years ago. Cheap grace has never left us; it is ever present, perhaps even in shiny new packages like the gospel-centered movement. It is the same perpetual lie of the comfort-seeking, worldly, nominal Western church: that one can make it to heaven without following Jesus in absolute surrender and genuine holiness. A crown without a cross.

Friend, make no mistake: only those who bear the cross will wear the crown.

The gate is small and the way is narrow that leads to eternal life (Matthew 7:14), and there are few who find it. We must constantly strive to enter through the narrow door (Luke 13:24).

We cannot avoid this tension because the New Testament does not avoid it.

The solution is to avoid shallow trends, and to return to the systematic and serious preaching of the entire New Testament, without apology, and let the chips fall where they may. Starting with the gospel of Jesus.

It is not too late to change.

PART TWO

What the Church is *Distracted By*

I.

The Great American Idol

THERE ARE SOME THINGS that the church is distracted by today. I want to address the one that is the most obvious.

Politics.

This is a big topic, but I believe we can say some very clear things about it in this little book.

Things that the church desperately needs to hear.

The entire world is aware of the chaos in our country. Some say our nation has never been more divided.

This division has crept inside the church.

It reveals both a problem and its solution.

I believe the problem is obvious: the church is not focused as it should be on the kingdom of Heaven. It is too focused on the kingdoms of earth; in this case, our own earthly kingdom, America.

Let's review a little theology. This will point the way toward the solution.

When Jesus came, he announced the arrival of a new kingdom; he called it the kingdom of God (Mark 1:15) or the kingdom of Heaven (Matthew 3:2).

This kingdom has begun its reign, but it will not be fully established until the end of all things, when Jesus comes again and brings an end to all earthly kingdoms.

The duty of all people is to strive to enter this kingdom; this is made clear throughout the teaching of Jesus. And followers of Jesus are to consider themselves citizens of this heavenly kingdom first and foremost and look forward eagerly to its fulfillment (Philippians 3:20). Above all earthly affairs, they should be about the business of this heavenly kingdom as their true priority.

Almost every Christian agrees with these truths; they are clearly stated in the New Testament.

How then are we in this predicament today?

How then are Christians dividing over the politics of our earthly kingdom?

How then are Christians depressed, discouraged, or angry when things in this nation don't go their way?

How then are Christians so overjoyed, elated, and satisfied when things in this nation do?

Something has gone wrong here.

Let's get back to the foundation–the person and work of Jesus.

II.

Jesus: Our Pattern

As we have seen in previous chapters, being a Christian means becoming a disciple of Jesus. It is to follow Jesus and take up his very life. To learn from him and imitate him.

Pause for a moment and think back once again to how Jesus lived his life. We have a fairly detailed record of it in the four gospel accounts.

What did Jesus think about on a daily basis? What did he say? What did he do?

What made him happy, sad, pleased, or disappointed?

Whatever it was, these are the same things that we should think about, talk about, and do.

It's very clear what occupied our Lord's life. It is on every page of the gospels.

The truth of God, which he taught or preached constantly.

And the love of God, which led him to seek out his fallen creatures.

This is what establishing the kingdom of Heaven looks like.

Jesus was consumed with his father's business. It was, as we have seen, his very food. And this is what we are to do.

This whole matter may be as simple as looking back through the New Testament to see if our lives look like what we see there.

Let's zoom in a little closer.

III.

Focusing on the Mission

THE FIRST THING ON Jesus's heart was the gospel; the good news that the kingdom of Heaven has come (Matthew 4:17).

Everywhere he went, he proclaimed it. Nothing is more obvious in the gospel accounts than this.

The gospel was to be proclaimed to the Jew first, and then to everyone else, as Paul puts it in Romans 1:16.

This is now our primary job. A fundamental duty of disciples of Jesus is to be witnesses of the gospel of Christ, wherever he places us.

This is the point of the Great Commission; making other disciples and teaching them to observe all that Jesus commanded.

A second task goes along with being a disciple: carrying the love of Jesus to the hurting and neglected.

In fact, these are the very ones who should get the gospel first. Jesus made this very plain at the beginning of his ministry (Luke 4:18–21).

Jesus ministered to the poor, the blind, the lame, and the demon-possessed. He sought out the outcasts and those weighed down by sin. He healed every kind of sickness and disease.

Jesus cared for the hurting. He made it his special mission to seek them out *first*.

This is to be our mission as well.

When we look at these two aspects, then being a disciple of Christ, a representative of the kingdom, begins to take on a whole new light.

Our mission as followers of Christ is actually quite simple.

Love and light. Wherever he places us.

This is how the kingdom of Heaven is spread.

How then does this relate to politics?

Quite directly, in fact.

IV.

What Do We Really Care About?

THE FIRST QUESTION TO ask ourselves here is simply this: do we care about the well-being of other people, just as Jesus did, or do we care about ourselves and our own interests?

I have found that many people are quite good at deceiving themselves on such questions; but still, the questions must be asked.

Do we care that people do not know God, love God, or serve God? Do we care that the hurting and sinners do not have God's love and light shared with them? Are we seeking out the lost and needy in our societies?

So much could be resolved in this matter if we were honest about our motivations.

Once again, the kingdom of Heaven is a future kingdom, and the whole point of earthly existence since Jesus has come is to *get into it*. This is the focus of all of Jesus's teaching. Nothing on earth matters other than becoming his true disciple.

We must consider this for ourselves, and, when we have gotten ourselves right, seek out others. This is the main business of the Christian.

Back then to earthly politics; all of our political involvement should come down to one simple question.

Why are we concerned with or involved in the politics of our earthly nation?

Are we concerned for ourselves or for others?

More to the point: are we involved for the sake of the kingdom of Heaven or for our earthly kingdom?

Nothing is more crucial than to resolve this issue of motivation here at the outset.

It really does come down to these simple issues.

My own life or others.

The kingdom of Heaven or my own kingdom.

Eternal, spiritual issues, or temporal, earthly ones.

Which one do I really care about?

Which one did Jesus care about?

I think the answer is obvious.

V.

Jesus and Earthly Nations

AMERICA IS AN AMAZING country in so many respects.

It is prosperous and powerful and has perhaps the most free-dom for its citizens of any country in history. Its form of govern-ment has been widely celebrated.

It makes sense that so many people, even around the world, love and appreciate it.

My wife, by contrast, grew up in a communist nation. She has seen firsthand the perils and horrors of 20th-century Marxism put into practice.

She and her family were dangerously poor and suffered re-ligious persecution. Eventually, her family was granted refugee status by the United States and allowed to live in our country due to the persecution they had faced.

Here, her father was able to work his way to earthly success. Within 15 years of coming to this country, he owned his own home in a prosperous neighborhood with money to spare. He could worship freely wherever he wanted.

He had lived the American dream—not the corrupt, greed-plagued version satirized by 20th century novelists, but the origi-nal, decent one—the dream of having the freedom to believe what you will and make an honest living with your own two hands.

In this respect, America is a great nation.

In other ways, of course, America is not a great nation. Its history is marked by the savage oppression of minorities, by brutal conflict—it nearly destroyed itself less than 100 years after its founding—and by some rather suspect foreign policy decisions and wars; and it remains as divided today as ever, as we said in the first chapter.

And yet—the point here is that it is easy to see how at least some people could love this country and want to preserve it.

What does Jesus think about America?

If the gospels are to be our guide, we have a clear picture of what Jesus thought about Rome, the great empire that ruled during his own earthly life. His attitude was simple: do what Rome is asking you to do. Pay your taxes. Do your duty. Don't cause a problem. There are infinitely more important matters to be concerned with.

This is exactly the same attitude Paul and Peter promote in their epistles. Obey the government, Paul says (Romans 13:1–7), for it is established by God. Obey the government, Peter says (I Peter 2:13–17), and thereby silence people who say foolish things about Christians (verse 15); in other words, don't give unbelievers an opportunity to say anything bad about you.

That's about it in the New Testament.

Jesus and his apostles didn't have much to say about earthly governments because they were too busy establishing the kingdom of God. This is clear and obvious in the Scriptures.

They came into conflict with the authorities, make no mistake. Once or twice they openly disobeyed to be obedient to their mission to preach the gospel, and ultimately they all suffered imprisonment and martyrdom.

But it was all for one purpose: the mission of Jesus, the kingdom of God. This was all they cared about.

So is it wrong to love an earthly nation? Is it wrong to care about it or even to try and protect or preserve it?

Certainly it is not sinful to love one's fellow countrymen or even one's country, but once again, this is the question we all must answer: what did Jesus and his disciples do? What occupied their time? What was their obsession? What was their daily motivation, their purpose?

I think we must all agree it was the kingdom of Heaven.

Nothing else mattered to them.

VI.

The Kingdom of Heaven and the Kingdoms of Earth

THE KINGDOM OF HEAVEN, again, is not of this world. Jesus made this plain (John 18:36).

The time of its full and final reign over all is in the future, when Jesus returns and brings an end to all earthly authority. This is also plain (I Corinthians 15:23–24).

It has no earthly borders and no earthly form of government.

It has no economic system or policies. It has no earthly laws or duties.

Its ruler is the Lord of the Old and New Testaments.

It will not be limited by space, time, or customs.

Again, as we have said, its purpose now, under the authority of Jesus, is to call all people to its obedience.

And it has no relationship to any present earthly government.

Let me repeat that.

The kingdom of Heaven has no relationship to any present earthly government.

The New Testament makes absolutely no statements or claims about any form of earthly government or any economic system. It is not concerned with these.

How then have so many American Christians blurred the lines? How then are they claiming that America is somehow God's special nation?

America has been established by God, but only in the sense that all earthly kingdoms have been, as Paul and Peter plainly tell us. Even the bad ones.

How then do American Christians claim that democracy and constitutional freedoms are either sanctioned or commanded by God?

Make no mistake–the coming of the kingdom of Heaven does bring freedom; the glorious freedom of Jesus.

Jesus came to free people from the kingdom of darkness, with its demonic hold over their souls and lives. He did so. But our freedom in Christ brings with it a new kind of bondage, a glorious one: a bondage to the Lordship and mission of Christ. Paul uses this imagery repeatedly in the New Testament.

It is true that Peter tells us to live as free people (I Peter 2:16) because of our freedom in Christ. And Paul says in another place that those who are bought by the blood of Jesus should not become slaves of men (I Corinthians 7:23) and should try to obtain their freedom if they are.

So the kingdom of Heaven does bring a freedom that has some application in the here and now.

But there are limits; and these limits keep us from getting too concerned with earthly matters. The life and ministry of our Lord Jesus and his apostles makes this clear, as we have seen.

It is likewise clear in the New Testament that full and final freedom from evil, or bondage, or oppression, is for our future heavenly kingdom.

It can be sought in the here and now, but never in such a way as to distract from the present mission of Jesus.

Always we must work for those in bondage and those who are oppressed; but again, there are limits. The kingdom of Heaven must always have priority; spiritual bondage and oppression must have priority as well.

Keeping our priorities in order is something all Christians need to diligently try to do.

As we know, it is not always that easy.

But my contention is that many American Christians have their priorities completely out of order.

VII.

A Practical Issue

HERE IS A THOUGHT experiment: would the apostles campaign and vote against abortion, if they were alive today?

Of course they would.

I hope it is obvious that I am not saying that being a follower of Jesus means never getting involved in politics.

Many political issues are also moral issues that directly impact lives. And as we all know, in the modern period of history, Christians in many countries have had a voice, a vote, in government.

Of course, then, Christians should be involved in politics. There are too many moral and social issues at stake.

But what is the goal?

Is it to save souls, or to save America?

Let's talk about abortion a bit longer. Few issues get as much attention in our day, and it serves as an interesting case study for our discussion.

What an incredibly horrible practice it is. It is hard to fathom how human beings could sink this low; to treat the miracle of human life as something that comes under the domain of mere personal preference.

To be sure, Christians should sympathize with women and mothers. It is true that so often in history women have had to bear the responsibility of carrying and rearing children while men are often able to get off completely free from such duties. And such horrific crimes as rape should be taken with the utmost seriousness and compassion.

But at the root of the abortion movement in our times, as we all know, are changing norms about sex. God never intended sex to take place outside the context of a loving, monogamous relationship between one man and one woman.

Make no mistake: abortion in our day and age is almost always an attempt to correct or erase the consequences of sin.

In the most perverse and despicable way.

Abortion should not be condoned in any situation, unless, of course, the mother's life is in real danger; then one might have moral grounds for taking life.

And Americans have a say in this.

Should Christians stand up and fight against pro-choice legislation?

Of course.

Should Christians get involved in helping those considering abortion?

By all means. Christians should be on the front lines of such battles.

But again, the motivation should be clear: it is because in God's eyes life is precious and must be protected. It is because in God's eyes the taking of life is wrong and should be opposed. It is because to stand up against evil, even public or social evil, is always right, though of course as followers of Jesus we do not do so by means of physical weapons or warfare.

It is not to protect and preserve our own society or way of life. And it is not to subversively promote the whole of our political agenda. I believe many Christians are doing this, perhaps without even realizing it.

It is to advance the kingdom of Heaven. To see more and more people believe in Jesus, follow Jesus, and live for Jesus. To see the truth of Jesus proclaimed and to help the needy and oppressed. To spread his love and light.

To everyone everywhere.

VIII.

Are We Guilty of Selective Empathy?

IF AMERICAN CHRISTIANS ARE interested only in their own country, let alone their own interests, they are missing the mark.

Again, the kingdom of Heaven knows no earthly boundaries or loyalties.

Jesus sent his disciples into all the world, to proclaim the gospel to all creation (Mark 16:15).

We are also to prioritize the poor, needy, and oppressed, just as Jesus did. All around the world.

To focus therefore only on America means that we do not share the vision of Jesus.

We are off mission.

Again, we must and should care for those around us, wherever God has placed us.

But this leads to another point: there *are* poor, needy, and oppressed people all around us, even in America.

Do we care for these?

There are so many in mental torment, in physical and emotional misery, right now, all around our country.

Do we care for these?

Unlike unborn babies, these face the possibility of eternal conscious suffering if they die apart from Christ.

Do we care for these?

There is a serious problem when abortion is the only issue we seem to have sympathy or compassion for. We have mentioned "selective theology," but having sympathy only for certain issues is something psychologists actually refer to as "selective empathy."

Selective empathy can occur when I am concerned about something that serves my own interests, not the interest of others.

Let me state it as plain as I can.

When I care for aborted babies, as I should, but not for the poor, the homeless, the refugee, the migrant, the addict, the sick, and the sinner, then I have an inappropriate—a sinful—selective empathy.

Campaigning fervently for abortion, as I have suggested, might actually conceal a hidden motive, which is to keep my country the way I like it.

Not caring for these other needy groups might serve the same purpose.

It all comes back to me and my interests.

I bring this very troubling possibility up only because I believe this may in fact be happening with many American professing Christians.

But this is precisely *not* what we see in Jesus in the gospel record.

Jesus didn't ask questions about sinners; he served them where they were.

Jesus didn't judge the truly poor or treat them like criminals; he helped them as he found them.

Jesus didn't limit himself only to certain causes.

Jesus was not plagued by self-interest.

His only concern was the will of God.

Again, I am not questioning the crusade against abortion. Of course we should stand against that.

I am questioning whether we truly have the genuine, full-orbed empathy of Jesus, produced by the Holy Spirit.

Once again, how odd it is that the ones who shout the loudest against abortion also seem indifferent toward the poor and the stranger—forgetting that all throughout the Bible, in the Old and New Testaments, we have constant commands to help these groups.

In fact, this was a great sin of the people of God in the Old Testament (Zechariah 7:9–14), something that God warned strongly against (Jeremiah 22:3).

Our Lord Jesus exemplified love and care for these groups of people. They were, as we have seen, his very mission.

Is it possible, then, that rather than having the genuine love and empathy of Christ, we are serving our own interests, our own agenda? That we are claiming to be acting in the name of Christ, when really we are trying to recreate a society we are comfortable with?

I believe it is quite possible, even probable, that this is happening.

This is one way I believe the American church has been distracted—even blinded—by politics.

IX.

Not God's Country

LET ME SAY IT again, as clearly as I can.

Our Lord Jesus does not have a special interest in the United States of America.

It is not his favored nation. There was one such nation, of course; it was the people of Israel in the Old Testament.

Now, with the coming of Jesus to earth, the entire world is to be called into God's kingdom. The kingdom of Heaven is the last great kingdom, the only one that matters.

This is why we cannot get too narrowly focused on one earthly country, no matter how much we love it.

Don't get me wrong; I think we can acknowledge that America was uniquely blessed by God. I think we can even say it has carried out a unique function in the modern world, especially when we consider such things as the evil threats of World War II, for example. In a sense, God has been behind all this.

In another sense, he has not.

America is not, nor ever could be, his people.

That is the now the universal church.

A reminder: church and state are now to be separate, because Jesus made it so. This idea was firmly established when he announced his heavenly kingdom and said it was not of this world.

This notion was not invented or discovered in Western countries in the modern period. It was finally accepted in the modern period, but it was first established by Jesus.

I fear this vital theological truth is under threat today.

Christians ought to know better.

But I want to be even more plain here.

The church does not need America. It does not need freedom or democracy. It never has.

Some might be troubled by this claim, but a sober look at both Christian history and the history of America have shown this.

God's church was born in a time of oppression. The first Christians were persecuted on a scale that was not repeated until perhaps the 20th century.

Christianity spread like wildfire during those early days. Within a few generations it had taken over Rome itself.

In the 20th century, it spread with unprecedented speed in countries like China, where it was actively opposed.

The gospel and the church don't need the protections of freedom and democracy because the Spirit of God cannot be hindered by earthly governments or policies. To say otherwise is blasphemy.

To be clear, no one would argue against the idea that some governments, systems, or periods of history are better than others. Paul told us to pray for kings and all in authority, that Christians would know peace (I Timothy 2:1–2). We should always pray against the oppression, persecution, imprisonment, and martyrdom of our fellow Christians.

But again, throughout history, the Spirit of God has often worked mightily during such times.

By contrast, during times of prosperity, the church has often grown soft and weak, allowing the culture to influence it.

I believe this has happened in our own country.

The proof might just be that we don't want to admit it.

X.

More on Forms of Government and Economic Policies

CONTRARY TO WHAT MANY American Christians claim today, the Bible does not endorse a certain form of government or economic system.

Neither does it endorse a particular political party.

How have we missed this?

The New Testament would never endorse a certain form of government because its concern is the kingdom of Heaven and the coming reign of Jesus.

The New Testament would never endorse a certain economic system because the duty of Christians is to lay up treasure in Heaven, not to be occupied with treasures on earth.

Again, how have we gotten this so wrong?

I believe it is clear that American society, American freedom, and American prosperity have tainted our thinking. Of course, I am by no means the first to suggest this.

Are there underlying biblical principles that might inform government systems or economic policies? Perhaps so. But it seems clear to me that how these are to be understood and applied is a complex matter indeed, far more complex than most American Christians are willing to admit.

Again, the New Testament takes no real interest in these matters.

Jesus said simply to pay taxes to the government (Matthew 22:21). Don't waste time thinking about it. Get on with the mission.

As we have seen, Paul and Peter say to obey the government as being established by God. Don't draw undue attention to yourself; be a peacemaker so that the real mission might go forward.

This is the very opposite of the American spirit.

America is a nation born of the desire for political and economic freedom. This cannot be disputed.

To protest certain issues peacefully–perhaps this is something Christians might do, if the oppression were truly severe.

But to rise up and rebel against the government because of it, in order to obtain political and economic freedom?

How absurdly contrary to the mission of Jesus.

This is why it is a bit bizarre to argue that America was a Christian nation, or that the founding fathers were on God's mission, or other such things one often hears in the Evangelical church today.

The very Lord of the universe, Jesus, cared nothing for these earthly things. His mission, as we have seen, was clear.

But somehow American Christians in alarming numbers have convinced themselves that God is on America's side, that it was and should be a Christian nation, or that we have to get our nation back to so-called Christian values.

I'm sorry to say it again, but political and economic freedom are not Christian values.

They have absolutely nothing to do with the kingdom of Heaven.

Jesus came to bind us to one mission: following him and doing his will.

Jesus called us to surrender everything to him, including our earthly possessions (Luke 14:33).

How dare we as Christians cling to our earthly freedoms and prosperity and cherish them! Jesus called us to give them up and become his servants.

The professing church in America has entirely lost sight of this call.

Let me make another claim that might sound outrageous to some Christians, but that might actually be the sober truth.

It seems to me that no one political party in our country is any closer to the ideals of the New Testament than the other. At least, not when considered on the whole.

One is loyal to Christian sexual ethics, but also to policies that unashamedly promote the pursuit of earthly wealth and prosperity, something absolutely abhorrent to Jesus.

The other has completely lost sight of Christian sexual ethics but seems more focused on the sharing of wealth and the needs of the poor and the stranger, both clear biblical ideals.

Whatever we might think of these claims, I think we should all agree that no Christian should have the audacity to claim that their political party is the one favored by our Lord.

Again, the party on the right is built on a platform of political and economic freedom; and this is the essence of our nation, the very makeup of it.

The great idols of it, I say.

The Holy Spirit has a different DNA, if you will: the same DNA in Jesus, our Lord and Savior.

It cares not for earthly freedoms or prosperity. It gives up all to reach the needy with the love and light of God the father.

It seeks to battle against the spiritual forces of evil, not those across the political aisle.

Its territory is the souls of men, not the borders of a particular country.

It cares not for self; it cares for God and others.

Its victory is salvation, now and on the day of judgement.

It looks beyond its own interests, its own future, its own country, and sees the needs of the entire world.

It asks: what can I give up for the kingdom of Heaven today?

XI.

The Root of the Idol

I SUGGEST THAT FOR many Christians, interest in politics may very well be nothing more than the overflow of a desire for what America has provided more than any other nation in history: the freedom to enjoy life the way we want.

In other words: the pursuit of earthly happiness.

This, after all, is the American way more than anything else.

The temptation that has gotten hold of society and the church is perhaps not really a political ideal after all.

It is money and pleasure.

This, then, is perhaps the greatest distraction of all in the church today: the enjoyment of life that our nation provides.

Jesus knew that this would be one of the greatest of all hindrances to following him.

That is why he talked about money so much, all throughout the gospel accounts.

"Watch out," he said, "and be on your guard against every form of greed" (Luke 12:15).

This is also why he demanded that we leave everything behind and follow him.

It is worth pointing out that the New Testament has a rather different view toward money and earthly possessions than the Old Testament.

The modern Evangelical church has so often failed to see this.

In the Old Testament, God often blessed his people with earthly wealth. This was a foundational way that God showed his favor. The Israelites were looking forward to an earthly paradise, a land flowing with milk and honey.

Now, we are looking forward to treasure in Heaven.

In the Old Testament, God commanded his people to be generous to the poor and give ten percent (a tithe) of all they had to the Lord.

By contrast, the New Testament ups the ante: *everything* is to be given to God.

This is a basic requirement of following Jesus, as we have seen. No man could be his disciple until he had first given up all his possessions and followed him.

In the early days of the church, the same principle was followed; no one said that anything was his own, but they had everything in common (Acts 4:32).

There is some additional explanation required here, of course.

The first believers were in the unique position of actually having to live together for a while. They had nowhere else to go after Jesus ascended to Heaven, and they were told to wait until the Holy Spirit fell on them. This is why they had all things in common.

But the principle in their example is timeless, and it is repeated throughout the New Testament. It is simple, really: following Jesus with all of one's being means that we truly let go of all that we are and all that we own.

We give them up from the heart first and foremost. We no longer desire them, and this means that we no longer seek them. We surrender them fully and dedicate our hearts and lives to the mission of Jesus, to loving God with everything within us.

This newfound call regarding money and possessions is a direct consequence of the coming of Jesus and the inauguration of his kingdom. With the coming of Jesus, the full and final will of God for our lives is revealed. The kingdom of Heaven is at hand.

This is why I say the issue of money in the New Testament is different than the Old.

In addition, the example of the early church shows what happens when the Holy Spirit truly fills a person. He surrenders all to Jesus; he no longer has any desire to own or cling to earthly things. His only thoughts are for God and others; he longs to share with those in need.

All true believers in Jesus have partaken of the Spirit in a new and powerful way. We have been born again (John 3:3). We are part of a new kingdom; we have a new calling, a new identity. Everything is new, and our attitude toward earthly things must change.

This is such a vital part of theology, but how often it goes missing in our churches!

Even when it is right in front of us in the New Testament.

Of course, none of us has been perfect in the use of money; none of us ever will be perfect in any area of our lives while we are on this earth. But stop and think about America for a while, and about our own lives in this bountiful country.

Has any group of people ever lived more comfortably in this life?

The temptations and dangers are real indeed.

And we have all been affected by them.

XII.

Treasures in Heaven

As I HAVE SAID, this nation was born of the idea that political and economic freedom were worth fighting and dying for. So many American Christians today seem to value these things to the same degree.

I think it is time to speak directly on this.

Really, follower of Jesus? Really?

Have you read your Bible recently? Have you seen the example of Jesus, and his teaching? Have you considered the disciples in the Book of Acts? Have you read the writings of the Apostle Paul, who said that with food and covering we should be satisfied (I Timothy 6:8)?

I think it could be argued that the American spirit, especially as it relates to our supposed right to earthly happiness, is actually *directly contrary* to the Spirit of Jesus.

Yet I have seen how easy it is to get caught up in it. Our levels of comfort and pleasure in America are unprecedented.

Most of us can afford to eat what we want, when we want; delicious, rich, elaborate meals. We can entertain ourselves in so many ways; movies, television, music, and a variety of things on the Internet. Most of us can take vacations when and where we want. We can choose the cars we want to drive and the houses we want to live in. And these cars and houses are usually far beyond what any thinking person would call "necessity."

And no one can tell us what to do about it. Not even our pastors.

No wonder so many people love America so much.

Don't get me wrong; having balance regarding money and possessions is often difficult. At this moment in our country, inflation has driven prices sky high. We have bills to pay and mouths to feed. We have our children's future to consider. And the high cost of medical care and insurance alone is something that weighs on everyone.

So I am not arguing, again, that we must literally sell everything we own and live together in a kind of commune with other believers. The New Testament calls us to work hard and provide for those under our care.

But it also calls us to a serious and very real sacrifice of our lives to the Lordship and mission of Jesus. And this will directly impact our money and possessions.

The key here, again, is the heart.

Are we truly seeking to love God with all our heart, soul, mind, and strength, as Jesus commanded? Then we will gladly surrender our lives, money, and possessions to his cause.

Our delight will not be in our own earthly happiness, or our own earthly prosperity, or our own earthly freedoms, or in our possessions.

We will truly rather give to others than spend on ourselves.

We will consider the poor and needy and make extraordinary sacrifices on their behalf.

We will give generously to the spread of the gospel around the world.

We will downgrade instead of upgrading.

We will avoid luxuries.

We will prayerfully consider what God would have us do with each dollar we make.

We will joyfully enter in to meeting the needs of the poor, starting with the people of God.

And in all of this, we will be storing up treasure in Heaven, not treasure on earth.

We will truly be following Jesus.

PART THREE

What the Church is *Confused About*

I.

Refocusing on the Mission

I WANT TO BEGIN this section by taking a closer look at the mission of the church.

It is clear in the New Testament, as we have already seen, that following Jesus means dedicating ourselves to his mission.

His mission, once again, is essentially this: spreading God's love and light in a dark and needy world.

Is the Evangelical church committed to this?

I think we can happily say that in many respects it is.

There are more Evangelical mission agencies than one can count. Some of these agencies have millions of dollars and have sent thousands of missionaries all over the world.

Not that it is enough, of course; the needs of the world today are vast. Millions upon millions are still without God's love and light. And as the world continues to grow, the need for missions will continue to grow as well. And yet, I believe it is fair to say that the church is doing a good job of trying to meet that need.

Some denominations, to be sure, are failing; I grew up in a denomination that was incredibly strong in the area of church life, but incredibly weak in the area of missions. Reaching the lost and needy with the gospel simply wasn't emphasized.

Thankfully, again, many denominations do emphasize it.

Does this mean that all is well in how the church is carrying out its mission?

I would have to argue no.

Just as our culture has affected so many other aspects of Christian life today, such as its doctrine and lifestyle, so too has it affected the area of mission.

Let me explain.

II.

Rethinking Missions

ONCE AGAIN, I THINK it is clear and undeniable that following Jesus means engaging in his mission. In his day, when one followed him and became his disciple, he knew it was his purpose to carry out the ministry of Jesus. His life and work would look like Jesus's.

During his earthly ministry, Jesus confirmed this by sending his disciples on regular mission endeavors to reach the lost. This is recorded in the gospel accounts.

After he died, we know what Jesus told us to do: he gave the church the Great Commission, the command to go into all the world and do what Jesus did, which is to spread God's love and light. And this is what his disciples did.

And this is what we must do. There is no other way to understand what being a disciple of Jesus means, as we have seen. This is not all being a disciple means, but it is an essential part.

But there's a catch.

This doesn't mean that everyone today is to leave everything behind and go be a foreign missionary.

What? Are we contradicting ourselves?

We are not. When the first disciples went into all the world to make other disciples, something new was formed. You know what this was.

The church.

Or, more specifically, local churches.

The first disciples, now called apostles, made it clear that wherever believers were found, they were to form a community. They were to gather each week for worship, mutual encouragement, prayer, and teaching and preaching. They were to meet each other's needs and work together to build each other up, each member using their unique spiritual gifts. This model is discussed all throughout the New Testament. This is the church.

If you think about it, it makes perfect sense that God would want his people to do this. But it is also incredibly instructive when it comes to his mission.

Here is what I mean: in any mission enterprise, the church is a sort of "end game." It is supposed to go like this: God sends workers out, the gospel is preached, people become believers and are baptized, and immediately they form churches and begin to grow. They learn to love and minister to each other in a way that pictures what Heaven will look like. They become, in each local area, the body of Christ, until we are all joined into that final body in Heaven.

At least two valuable lessons come from this model.

First, there is no successful biblical mission unless a thriving, functioning church is the result.

Second, there is a new way in which missions is to take place in the church age–it must go through the church.

I would argue that the current Evangelical church has failed to properly consider both of these points.

III.

Slowing Down the Process

ONE OF THE MOST dangerous trends in missions today is something called "rapid church-planting."

So-called missionaries go from place to place and plant as many "churches" as they can, as quickly as they can.

This is simply not the biblical model. It is also, for lack of a better word, foolhardy.

To make matters worse, some missionaries, it seems, fail to understand at all how important the church is.

They fail to see that the church is God's end plan for missions. Merely trying to get as many people as we can to believe in Jesus is not the end goal. If this were the case, practically the entire New Testament from Romans on would not have been written. All these books were written so that Christians might grow individually and collectively in their local churches.

So one of the first things to do in missions is to acknowledge how important the church is. Without it, Christians cannot grow. Without it, Christians might not endure to the end. It is vital, both from God's perspective and from ours.

God's goal, as we have seen, is not mere intellectual acceptance of Jesus. It is discipleship.

One must commit to it from the beginning, but its full expression involves a lifetime of growth in holiness, what theologians call sanctification. And this requires the church: its preaching, teaching, fellowship, and various ministries.

Those who fail to emphasize the church, then, fail to understand not only missions, but what following Jesus means.

Another thing to reflect on here is what the church should look like. Several churches in the New Testament were famously weak. They had failed to properly understand or apply the apostles' teaching, and they were plagued with sin issues.

The apostles labored endlessly to see them grow. Again, they didn't just leave them alone. Paul compared it to laboring in childbirth until mature, Christlike believers were formed (Galatians 4:19).

This means that at the very least, churches need to have mature, blameless leaders to oversee and teach the flock. Churches also need to stand for the truth (I Timothy 3:15), being faithful to proclaim God's Word without apology. They need to provide opportunities for spiritual gifts and ministries to be exercised and to apply discipline where needed. Again, these things are clear in the New Testament.

If these things are not in place, the mission is not finished. Period.

But how should we expect American missionaries to take the church this seriously, when so few are taking it this seriously at home?

IV.

Missions: A High Calling

AGAIN, I WOULD ARGUE that if there are not mature men available to install as leaders, then the mission effort is not complete. If there is not faithful teaching and preaching, it is not finished. The same with faithful ministry, worship, and discipline.

These things take time and are difficult.

Two things that Western culture no longer has tolerance for.

And this leads to the second lesson from the church age: there is a new way in which mission endeavors are to be undertaken.

When Jesus called all people to be his disciples, he really did call everyone to become his witnesses for all of life. This part is clear.

In the church age, however, it is clear in the New Testament that new believers are not to become full-time missionaries right off the bat. The first task of new believers is to get into local churches, begin to grow spiritually, and then to exercise their spiritual gifts.

Of course, all believers, at every stage, are to be witnesses for Christ where he has placed them. This is part of discipleship, and, I would argue, the natural result of the supernatural work of God in a person's soul.

But this is not a missionary.

A missionary in the Bible is one who is sent by God to fulfill the unique task of preaching the gospel, planting churches, and doing good in a specific place. Not everyone is called to this ministry.

The primary role in missions, then, is that of a "church-planter," a man who is specifically prepared, called, and anointed by God for this unique ministry.

Do American Evangelicals understand how significant this calling and ministry are? I am not sure they do.

Another thing we need to recover, then, is an understanding of the primary role of the true missionary, the one who is sent to plant new churches in areas where there are none. In the New Testament record, there is really no other kind of missionary. There are those called alongside this man to help him, but this role cannot be replaced or substituted. And certainly no new mission effort should be undertaken without this man leading the way.

Another, and arguably even more important thing, is to recover some biblical sense of the notion of maturity, as well as the seriousness of the call to ministry.

It is my settled conviction that American culture on the whole is incredibly shallow. We are no longer a sober, reflective, inquiring, knowledgeable people. We have few deep thoughts, no education of any real depth or breadth, and no appreciation for truth or beauty. We truly are a "pop" culture, and this shallowness has undoubtedly taken over American Evangelicalism.

In the church, as we have said, we have lost sight of who God really is and what he requires of us.

This can be seen in our choice of ministry leaders and in how we rush the ministry process.

Ministers in the Bible had to go through a period of growth, maturity, and refinement. This was God's preparation in their lives. The goal of this process is to be pure for the anointing of the Holy Spirit.

With Moses, this took 40 years. With Paul, it was a decade before he was called to his special work of missions. Even Timothy, a special case due to his youth, was at least 30 years old, according to biblical scholars, and likely in his mid-thirties.

God's work of preparation in the souls of his prospective ministers cannot be rushed.

And it is the job of church leaders to oversee this process.

I would argue that in many cases we are failing.

How in the world is it that so many of our pastors are young men in their mid-twenties? Those who have no life experience? Who have not been tested? Who have not been seasoned?

How is it that men are being allowed to become pastors after merely graduating from seminary and going through a brief internship? How can such a man lead the people of God?

How is it that young couples or those otherwise unqualified for serious ministry roles in our churches at home are sent out as missionaries, sometimes as lead missionaries? Those who haven't yet overcome their ambition, jealousy, worldliness, covetousness, and immorality? Who do not yet have the spiritual disciplines firmly in place? I have seen scores of such unprepared people; I have been one myself.

Where is our sense of patience, of growth, of maturity?

Like everything else in our culture, we want things to be done *now*.

But God's plan and God's way cannot be rushed.

American mission efforts need badly to reform—in our understanding of the importance of the church, in our understanding of the importance of the church-planter, and in our understanding of the place and importance of growth and maturity in our potential missionaries.

It is high time to stop sending unprepared workers to do serious spiritual work.

There *is* a place for younger, less-seasoned believers to come alongside and help church-planters, as we have said, provided they are of proven preparation, calling, and spiritual giftedness for their task. Again, the work of missions is not limited to church-planting by any means. Many may come alongside and help the church-planter. There are all sorts of needs on the field and all sorts of roles to be filled.

But everyone, I would argue, must have a clear sense of calling, preparation, and maturity.

And the church must be seriously involved in this process; and they must take it with the utmost seriousness.

Not missions agencies, of course; these can be helpful, but they must never lead the way. Qualified pastors, men in charge in local churches who are themselves holy, mature, and seasoned; these are God's appointed leaders in this task, and the congregation must come alongside and help them.

God help us to recover these biblical standards!

V.

The Whole World Reconsidered

THERE IS ANOTHER THING to consider in the work of missions: its scope.

And this has particular application to us Americans.

Some of this will touch on the same ground we covered in the previous section, on politics. But it really belongs here, because this is not a political issue. It is of vital interest to the mission of Jesus.

Jesus called us to go into all the world. This is part of leaving everything behind to follow him.

It also reveals the scope of the kingdom of Heaven.

It is open to everyone, in every nation.

The entire world.

For now on, then, our mission in life, as Christ-followers, is to think about nations other than our own.

We don't hear about this much.

As we have already said, most people are concerned about their own nation. Perhaps nowhere is this more true than in America.

Fellow Christian, what about the kingdom of Heaven? What about your future brothers and sisters, your fellow citizens, in other countries? Are you considering them?

American Christians simply *must* enlarge their thinking. The call of Christ to discipleship, which culminates in the Great

Commission, is in a very real sense a call to focus more on the kingdom of Heaven, and not on one's own earthly kingdom. It is to think about the spread of the gospel around the world.

And it is to target, in particular, the same ones Jesus targeted: the poor, the needy, and those who have never heard the gospel. Even if they are in other countries.

And in our day, it is clear: the poorest and least spiritually advantaged people live outside of the United States.

So here are some questions to consider.

What is the state of the world regarding knowledge of the gospel?

How about churches in other countries? Are they growing and maturing, or are they still in need of help?

Where are the greatest needs? Which countries need Jesus or spiritual help the most?

Let's be honest: America has had its chances. America has had as much gospel light as any nation in modern history.

Countries with the least amount of light should be prioritized.

Friends, America will pass away. The kingdom of Heaven will last forever.

America might crumble before our eyes. So what, if the church is in tatters?

Christian culture in America might forever be lost. Why should we despair, when some cultures have never been even remotely Christian?

Christian truth is still everywhere in our country. It is unavoidable. It is encountered on our television screens, social media, news outlets, and, of course, in a church near you.

What about places that still have never even heard the name of Jesus?

Let's be clear; I am not arguing that we should not care at all about what is happening in our country, as I said before. My response to the problems in our country is twofold. First: we must remember that the goal, and the solution, is not outward, political, or cultural. It is always inward and spiritual. Second: as we have said, we cannot care more about American culture than we do about the kingdom of Heaven. To do so would be to be disloyal to our calling as followers of Jesus.

I believe this means we should work toward caring about the needs of the whole world–Christians and unbelievers–as much as we do those of our own nation.

Even more.

Jesus started in Jerusalem. So did the apostles. This was God's will in the flow of redemptive history.

But then they turned their attention to the Gentiles, the whole world, of which America is a part. And then they moved on to nations that had not heard.

This is the scope, or even the essence, if you will, of the Great Commission.

We must do the same. Especially, again, because America has had so much spiritual light–and still does.

Let's consider some practical questions once again:

Do I know or care about the state of the church in, say, India, a nation over four times the size of my own? Do I know how it is struggling? Do I know the battles and dangers Christian pastors there are facing? Does this bother me?

What about other countries? Am I aware of the struggle, even the persecution, that believers are facing in certain places? Does this trouble me?

Do I care that whole language groups still don't have a gospel witness?

Do I know how many people die apart from Jesus each day in certain countries, such as Africa?

Do I even really care when people die without knowing Jesus?

Am I aware of the needs of the larger unbelieving world? Their disadvantages, both spiritual and physical? Their lack of food and water? Their poverty and diseases? Their social turmoil?

Am I actually thinking about the kingdom of Heaven?

Or am I still thinking about my own earthly kingdom–or, perhaps more accurately, myself?

VI.

A Mission of Love

I WANT TO SPEAK a bit more about the scope of missions, though what follows also relates to its task.

I have said that the mission is simple and reflects the ministry of our Lord Jesus.

Love and light.

Few Christians, churches, or mission groups hold these in proper balance today.

There's a reason: race relations, social justice, and similar issues have caused turmoil in our congregations.

In some places they have divided them.

This issue needs to be addressed.

First, a few more words on love and light.

It is clear that love—and by love here, I mostly mean caring about people's hurts and needs—is something that strongly motivated Jesus.

As we have said, it's displayed on every page of the gospel record.

His apostles were concerned with this also; they created a new church office (deacon) to care for people's physical needs, and as Peter, James, and John reminded Paul, they were to care for the poor even as they preached the gospel (Galatians 2:9–10).

Powerful stuff.

Individual Christians, then, as followers of Jesus, should always care for those in need, both within and without the church. It's clear: physical hurts and needs matter greatly to our Lord.

And this is also to be the church's mission.

How is the church doing on this?

It's hard to say, but I have to confess that at times I fear it is failing.

Think about the poor around the world; do we care about them enough to help them? With at least our money and prayers? Or do we only care about others if it serves our self-interest?

At this moment, my family's NPO is involved in helping hundreds of refugee orphans who are caught up in a horrible civil war in Myanmar. As I write this, we have just heard that dozens of them might have been lost in a devastating flood. The rest face disease, deprivation, and the constant danger of errant bombs.

Most people don't even know this war is going on, because the focus of our nation is on our allies—those who serve our interests.

Jesus knows about Myanmar.

Do you think Jesus cares as much or even more—perhaps far more—about what is happening in Myanmar, a country that has never had our physical or spiritual advantages, than he does what is happening in our country?

I think the answer is clear.

If we were honest, the truth is that we don't think about those in other countries very often, especially those who don't serve our interests.

This brings me to certain groups here at home.

What is your attitude toward the poor in our country?

Most people are content to pass them by or blame them for their own sin.

Surely, we say, this person deserves to be in the situation they are in. Surely, we argue, this person could have avoided this misery.

Jesus never asked questions of the poor.

He met them where they were, no questions asked.

He called them to repentance–don't get me wrong. Jesus never left someone in their sin.

But he was sympathetic and ministered to all.

Do we have this kind of compassion?

Let's bring it even closer to home.

What about certain minority groups in our culture?

What about immigrants trying to gain a better life for themselves?

Let's just go all the way: what about those who are hostile toward our Christian beliefs? Those across the political aisle?

Jesus said to even love our enemies.

All of these are to be targets not of our hatred, or our disregard, or our insults, but of our love, care, and kindness.

I fear that we so often do not know what spirit we are of (Luke 9:55).

VII.

The Social Justice Issue

I AM NOT SAYING the social situation is not difficult today, especially with things like the so-called social justice movement. This issue has divided the church as much as anything. Even as I write these words, there is serious division taking place inside not just the Evangelical church, but just one part of it, the part that leans toward Reformed theology. Over just this one issue.

Is it possible both sides have it a bit wrong?

I think it is.

Let me try to explain where I am coming from as simply as possible.

Any time a group of people feel oppressed, mistreated, or hurt by others, the offending party must—I repeat, must—consider their actions, seek to repent where necessary, and work hard to appease the offended party. Even when they think they are not in the wrong, they must be sympathetic and listen.

This is basic Christianity.

Are white Christians doing this today with their black brothers and sisters?

Perhaps some are, but on the whole, I do not think the response is adequate.

It's not history I am talking about. That part is inexcusable. Of course white Christians must be sensitive to what our forefathers were guilty of in the past and how that continues to have ramifications to this day.

I am speaking of the injustices and oppression that exist today.

I am not saying we should turn a blind eye toward things like critical race theory.

It is clear that this is a theory of the unbelieving world, influenced by the ideas of Marx, who was so very obviously set against Christianity.

But is it possible that some people have made it too big of a deal? Is it possible that anxiety over this theory has been used by the devil?

I believe it is.

Those who are angry about "woke" Christians are quick to claim that these have been fooled by the world.

I think the opposite may be true. I think it is those who are nervous about such things as CRT that have been fooled. They are so entrenched in their American ways that they have almost completely lost sight of what following Jesus should look like.

How dangerous is this theory really? Is it a theory that threatens to drive us to sin? Forsake God? Go the way of the world? End up missing out on God and Heaven?

Not really. It is a theory that advocates something far less serious: the shake-up of our present social order. The earthly rule of the oppressed rather than the oppressor. The loss of personal property, perhaps.

All things Jesus never cared about.

How can we be overly concerned about this theory when souls are dropping off into eternity moment by moment?

Christian reaction to this theory has in many cases bordered on the absurd.

Is Marxism really a more dangerous idea to our spiritual well-being than any other economic theory?

I put it to you that only someone who is earthly-minded would believe so.

Again, I am not trying to downplay the rise of such theories.

I am just arguing that the church has overreacted to them. Quite badly, in fact.

Once again, it makes you wonder where our priorities are.

Yes, Marxism's ultimate goal is to get rid of private property. Marx made this plain in his *Communist Manifesto*. I know well, because I studied and taught the text for years.

Why should this overly concern us?

Early Christians surrendered their private property joyfully (Hebrews 10:34).

No earthly loss can take away our faith, hope, and joy—if these are truly God-given.

We really have lost our spiritual moorings.

This is yet another moment in our country's history, I would argue, that clearly shows how tainted the American church is with earthly ideas. This deception is far deeper than any supposed "woke" deception. It has been going on in this country for generations.

I put it to you that critical race theory, or even Marxism, is not our enemy any more than, say, capitalism is. In fact, it could be argued that the latter system—the one so prized by Americans—is more dangerous to genuine, inner spirituality than its various counterparts. We know that the love of riches and pleasure can lead us to spiritual destruction; the Bible makes this plain.

I lived for years in a country where Marxism had completely won. Christianity thrived during its darkest years. Some would argue that it is growing weaker in this country of late, as the influence of capitalism grows.

Is genuine, biblical Christianity thriving in America?

VIII.

Not Like Jesus Enough

I WANT TO SAY it again: I think the whole critical race theory issue has been horribly overblown in the church.

Certainly denominations should not have considered adopting it as a framework. We have no framework but the Word of God.

But I happen to know of three separate situations in which church leaders were working to promote minorities into positions of leadership in their churches, simply out of concern to better reach a certain segment of their church population and their surrounding area, as well as to promote more unity and equality among the different groups represented in their churches. Because of the noise about critical race theory, each attempt failed. Spectacularly.

In one case, most church members left. In the others, the congregation voted the measures down overwhelmingly.

What's wrong with us?

Would Jesus care about the oppression of minority groups? Would he be interested in bringing unity and equality to our church leadership and our congregations? Would he be eager to reach certain less represented groups?

How can we even ask that question? The entire New Testament, from the ministry of Jesus to the writings of the apostles, in particular the apostle Paul, makes it clear that racial reconciliation and unity are among the most treasured end results of the gospel. And as we have seen, Jesus made it a special point to reach the oppressed in society.

I submit it to you that the white majority today, including those in the church, have not adequately thought about the difficulties of being a minority. This is not even to consider the question of the horrific past of certain minority groups in our country.

I have worked with minorities for years in various countries.

Where there are multiple people groups together, especially if one group is clearly in the majority, racism and oppression always persist. These things are embedded in the sinful human heart.

Christians, then, must work doubly-hard against these things. We must show every effort to overturn them. We must lock arm-in-arm with those in the minority and show them that we will stand with them. We have to; it is our calling as followers of Jesus.

Jesus–who was the first and greatest to break down the walls of racism and oppression. Go back and read through the gospel accounts.

Consider this as well: Jesus told us that *we* would be oppressed; that any who follow him would be. Go read again the Sermon on the Mount. If we are truly following Jesus, we will be poor in spirit, we will mourn, we will be meek, we will be persecuted, we will be insulted.

Just as he was.

And here we are getting to the heart of the matter.

It may be that white Christians are not standing with minority groups because white Christians themselves are not oppressed or persecuted enough.

In other words, we are not like Jesus enough.

We have not truly left everything behind to follow him.

We still love our freedoms, comforts, property, and pleasures too much.

We have pursued prosperity and fear its loss above all else.

This is why we don't wish to hear about oppression.

It scares us.

But really, only one thing should scare us: disobeying Jesus.

Here is the question for the White Christian church:

Where are the minorities in your congregations? Do you even have any?

Are you working to make all kinds of people feel accepted in your churches?

Are you willing to repent of your neglect and unconcern?

Are you willing to listen to your minority brothers and sisters?

Are you willing to let go of your prejudgments—your prejudices?

Are you more concerned about the loss of your freedom, comforts, and belongings than you are the presence, power, and pleasure of God?

Than unity and equality in the church?

Than justice all around you?

Are you truly a follower of Jesus?

Or are you simply an American Christian?

IX.

A Word to the Oppressed

BUT THERE IS ANOTHER side to this matter.

And here we must speak the truth to those who feel oppressed.

The impossibly despicable treatment of Africans in the modern era, by the entire Western World, is truly beyond understanding. It was exploitation of the worst possible kind–in the name of economic prosperity.

The same can be said about our own country's treatment of African Americans, of course.

Not only before "emancipation." After it as well.

I believe this mistreatment continues to this day in many forms.

No doubt it is better now than it was years ago, but even so, the effects of 400 years of abuse and oppression cannot be erased in a few decades.

And as I have said, minority groups will always suffer, often in subtle ways.

My dear minority friend: you have been the victim of oppression. Perhaps in many ways you still are.

You see the mistreatment of your black brothers and sisters, and it grieves you to the core.

No wonder some of you have left white-majority churches.

But what would Jesus have you to do?

There is a word here for you as well.

There is no doubt that Jesus came to loosen the bonds of oppression.

Make no mistake, he would never go so far as to shed blood or wage war over the issue; to say otherwise would be blasphemous. He will carry out his own judgement upon men finally and fully in the future, when he comes again.

But still, he would care, and he would work on your behalf. Jesus came bringing life, freedom, and peace to all.

He would certainly stand with you in your suffering.

He would protest with you.

He would rally to your support.

He would speak out on your behalf.

He would condemn the injustice of others toward you.

He would purge his people of any remaining sin in this area. He would weave a whip of cords and drive out the hypocrites from his church—those who have made prosperity their idol. We should not go this far, of course; but as King of Kings and Lord of Lords, he could.

But I believe he would also tell you this incredibly important message:

Don't forget about the real mission.

Don't forget about the kingdom of Heaven.

Don't get so focused on the here and now, even on your own very real suffering, that you forget your true purpose.

To show the love and light of Jesus.

To suffer with joy if need be, as we have mentioned.

To not go so far in your push against authorities, that an outsider might speak evil against Christians.

To keep your heart fixed on forgiveness and unity.

To look above all else to that heavenly city, built for you by God himself, where you have an eternal inheritance (Hebrews 11:10).

Of course it is difficult to do all this. But I would remind you: Christians have suffered since the beginning of our Lord's earthly life. None more than Jesus himself. And all those who believe must follow in his footsteps. This is what he called us to.

Once more, just so we are clear, it is not wrong to seek your own freedom from oppression; to try and improve your life in peaceful ways. As we have seen, Paul said we should seek this because we have been set free by Christ.

But never in a way that distracts from the mission.

You see, oppressed people must be on mission too. In fact, it is often in times of oppression that the Spirit of Jesus shines most brightly and purely.

Even oppressed people must not exchange heavenly hopes and joys for earthly ones.

For after all, this carrying of the cross, this narrow road, is the only path to Heaven.

X.

Beginning Again on Missions

Is IT IMPOSSIBLE TO find balance on this issue?

I don't think so.

Is unity in the church impossible?

Again, I don't think so.

But unity will require more than just getting our congregation to focus on "missions." I have been in churches where they thought a Great Commission focus would solve everything.

It didn't. It's possible to be focused on the Great Commission—on getting the gospel to the ends of the earth—and still not be following Jesus at home.

I have seen people give a great deal of money to missions and still keep storing up treasures on earth.

I have seen missions pastors embroiled in regular sin and have to step down.

I have seen churches where hundreds are going overseas but nobody is praying for them.

Being on mission is far more than "missions."

It means doing God's will in every area of life, right where you are.

And that might mean, somewhat paradoxically, *not* going overseas to work in missions.

I learned this the hard way. I went overseas as a young, single man, thinking I would never return.

I was far too immature to be there. After four years, I came home to try and grow up a little.

A few years later, I returned, this time married and more mature.

But then, after only a few years of blessed ministry, God sent us home. For no reason we could think of.

I've been in America ever since.

I am proof that God doesn't want everyone on the mission field.

But we also see this is the Bible.

Let me attempt to paint the picture once again, a little more carefully this time, of how the church today should obey Jesus in regard to overseas missions. Here are the steps.

First, we must make sure there are godly, mature leaders in place in our home churches, who will unapologetically preach and apply all the truth in the Bible. The congregation must consistently be pointed to holiness and right living. 2 Timothy 4:2–5 beautifully states how vital this ministry is.

I should point out again that the Great Commission is not complete *in your own church* unless this is in place!

Second, make sure your church is a place of regular, consistent, intercessory prayer, which is prayer for all those in need, Christians and non-Christians.

The entire church should engage in this regularly.

It is an incredible shame that this isn't happening in our churches. We can worship all night. But no one can pray.

Yet it is in an atmosphere where both are happening that the Lord sets apart those he has called for ministry (Acts 13:2).

This is perhaps an appropriate time to mention the hand-raising trend.

Everyone is doing it.

In the Old Testament, where we first see it, it is mostly a sign of prayer. Sometimes worship, but mostly prayer.

Here then is my comment on the worship and hand-raising movement.

I pray for a revival of the "lifting up of holy hands" in prayer in our churches (I Timothy 2:8). If this isn't happening, then I believe it is likely that the modern worship movement is not of God. Prayer is just that important in the Bible.

Those who don't pray regularly and urgently will not be holy, and they will not be used of God.

Along these lines, third, we must make sure that there is both an adequate pipeline for prospective missionaries and an adequate process to test their maturity (I Timothy 3:10). A study of the entire Bible, again, shows that this kind of preparation and testing is something God does with every minister of his, no matter how humble their ministry.

Finally, we must make sure the entire congregation knows what missions is supposed to look like, especially those interested in going to another culture to either plant churches or assist in a mission effort there.

This leads us back to where we started this chapter.

Again, God doesn't want everyone overseas. He calls particular people to unique ministries.

He wants everyone first to be holy in character and practice.

To be on mission, truly, means honoring God in every area of life.

Everyone should be involved in missions, indeed; but this begins with holiness and prayer. And achieving real growth in these areas takes time. Lots of it.

Then, everyone should be consistently involved with ministries of love and light wherever they are, starting with the body of Christ. They should also seek to put into practice their spiritual gifts within the body. Everyone should have the opportunity to do so.

Then we will see how God will work, and whom he will call to other ministries.

Let me end this section with a particular word to young people.

Young person—especially if you are a new convert, but even if not—don't be so eager to engage in overseas missions!

As I mentioned, Paul called Timothy "youthful," but he was at least 30 years old, Bible scholars believe.

The lesson here is that ministry, especially gospel ministry, is not for the spiritually immature and untested.

It is war, only for those who have been trained for battle. Or those who are battle-tested.

Sadly, our mission fields are often being populated by young and unproven people.

I know well. I was such a person, and I have seen many others. This should not be.

Such believers should stay home, grow, and learn to pray.

Young Christian, go to college. Get as much education as you can, or you think you might need. Do it now, before you do anything else. College and graduate school are a great time to grow up.

Settle the marriage question if possible. Give the devil as few weaknesses to exploit as possible.

Go through the preparation process. Don't allow a missions agency to expedite it. Let your elders lead you.

And seek to gain as sober an understanding of your spiritual gifts–and your limitations–as possible.

Remember that in a very real sense, God doesn't need you over there. A few people filled with the Spirit are worth a thousand who aren't. This is what the apostles in the book of Acts show us.

Above all, learn to pray, consistently and accurately, for mission endeavors and for national churches struggling to survive on the field. Prayer for missions is more important than all else, and it is not being done.

Remember that God desires to be glorified in us wherever we are. This is our ultimate calling.

Stay a while in this situation. Grow, pray, build; your own life and your family's. Learn to be faithful. Grow in humility, the most foundational grace of all. Wait on God.

Then—watch out.

The Spirit just might call you out (Acts 13:2).

XI.

Gender and Sexuality

I WANT TO TURN briefly now to another issue the church is confused about.

The issue of sexual morality.

Thankfully, most Evangelical churches are holding the line on the critical issues of homosexuality and gender.

Let me speak first to those who might be tempted to think differently.

God's will regarding sex and gender is clear.

Man and woman are sacred biological categories to him. This is seen from Genesis to Revelation. The evidence is so clear and strong that there is really no need to review it here.

Sexual relations are also sacred. In the sex act, among other things, the God-ordained sanctity of the male and female distinction is emphasized. Man and woman come together to create life.

But as we all know, in our modern era we have exchanged traditional, objective values for subjective ones. If I *feel* like doing something, I should do it. If I am *inclined* a certain way, I should embrace it.

We cannot give up the clear teaching of the Bible based on our feelings.

I realize that the issue of homosexual feelings and identity is no small matter for some. Romance and sex are perhaps the most powerful of all human experiences and pleasures.

But therein lies part of the problem. It is fairly obvious that our culture has given sex and the emotions far too important a place, at least during the last few centuries.

Don't get me wrong; human beings have struggled with God's design for sex and marriage since the beginning.

Think of Sodom and Gomorrah. Think of ancient Greece and Rome. Homosexual behavior, along with all kinds of other perversion, was widespread.

In the modern period of history, the period after the Renaissance and Reformation (the end of the Middle Ages), Western societies slowly moved away from their Christian origins into humanism. A change in sexual ethics is expected.

When principles in society begin to lose their value, and our social contexts no longer expect or require certain things of us, is it any wonder that our feelings and instincts become primary?

Thus, if I have certain desires, I should act on them.

Mind you, sexual immorality in our day is not limited to the homosexuality issue.

Marriage in general has been cast to the side. People live together regularly. People change partners regularly.

When marriage does happen, affairs are common. Divorce is widespread. And perversion and even sexual crime are everywhere.

All of this shows that human beings have lost their moorings. But to be governed by our feelings is hopeless and pointless. There are no limits, no boundaries.

Morality cannot be merely subjective.

But let me go deeper, just for a moment.

Most people are unaware that their feelings are the result of a variety of complex factors.

It is not simply genetics or nature. Nurture—how we are raised—also plays a crucial part. The formation of our psychology from a young age is critical.

No wonder our young people are struggling with these issues today.

We are rearing them in a confusing, chaotic, perverse society. All moral standards have been cast to the side.

How then is it that we are okay with allowing young people, even children, to decide such foundational things as sexual preference and gender identity? When they are raised in a society without any recognized moral norms?

And when their brains, personalities, and behavior are still developing, as we all know?

We don't treat them as adults in other things. We let them get away with murder, for Heaven's sake. Yet somehow we give them complete autonomy and authority on such critical issues as gender identity and sexual preference.

When they do something we find heinous, we tell them, *but you are just a child.* When they do something we find acceptable, we say, *you should be treated like an adult.*

It truly is absurd.

Without a doubt, our feelings, especially about sex, are *ruling* our culture.

Not God. Not religion. Not morality. Not any kind of propriety. Not history and tradition of any kind.

Sexual pleasure has become our one true God.

I'm not sure it can get any lower.

Step one for those struggling with this issue, either personally or intellectually, is this:

We must realize how far we have sunk, and how dangerous our times are.

Step two is to get back to the Bible.

If we believe the Word of God is true, we must stick with it.

It is our only hope.

XII.

Some Practical Suggestions

HERE ARE SOME ADDITIONAL suggestions.

First, we must take all sexual sin, including the sin of homosexuality, with the utmost seriousness.

It is of course true that such sins have been with us since the beginning. It is of course true that there are other sins that are equally grievous, and in fact much more so, than sexual sins.

And yet, we must recall that this particular sin is mentioned by Paul in the first chapter of Romans as a key sign that God has in some serious sense given over a society.

Think about that for a moment.

If you are still holding on to the idea that God is with our country, or that his influence is still strong in this country, let's be clear.

It isn't.

We cannot compromise on this issue. We have to preach against it unapologetically.

At the same time, we have to deal compassionately with those struggling in this area. We cannot treat them as strange, weird, inferior, dangerous, or any such thing.

We have to treat them as Christ treated all sinners, including the most notorious. We have to treat them with the same sensitivity that Jesus had.

Without compromising our stance on the matter.

Is it possible to hold these two attitudes in balance? To regard the sin with the utmost seriousness, and the sinner with the utmost sensitivity and compassion?

We have to, because Jesus did.

Let the world despise us for our stance on sexual matters. Let them judge and even reject us. Let them call it hate.

It is not hate; it is love. Love to God first, and then love to man.

Are we willing to accept the rejection of the world?

This issue may very well become a sort of litmus test of Christian faithfulness. It might be that already. Are you willing to stand with God on this issue and suffer the rejection of the world? Even the loss of potential friendships or career opportunities?

It is all just part of following Jesus.

XIII.

A Controversial Question

THERE IS ANOTHER QUESTION on this issue worth addressing briefly. It has come up again and again on social media.

Can a Christian be gay?

The answers from many have confusing.

Some say no, wondering how one could claim to be a follower of Jesus and still experience certain feelings and desires.

Others say yes, arguing that certain instincts may simply be part of one's nature, and not necessarily sinful.

I believe the former position is the correct one; but I will add a caveat.

The second group is fond of arguing that homosexual orientation is an essential part of someone's identity, and therefore not sinful in and of itself.

But of course it is sinful to be oriented toward homosexuality.

One doesn't need to argue, as Christians were fond of arguing in the past, that homosexuality is a choice. It is now widely accepted that very few gay people see their orientation as a choice; no doubt in a very real sense it is not.

This is not the point.

Homosexual orientation might be part of a person's essential makeup. But our essential makeup is not therefore sinless. It is mixed with sin through and through. "In sin did my mother conceive me," David writes in Psalm 51:5.

This is the same writer who said that God knit him together in his mother's womb (Psalm 139:13).

These two verses do not contradict each other. God oversees the creation of each new person, but as a result of the Fall, he allows the effects of sin to play their part.

We are still created in his image, but unlike the first humans, that image is now marred and intermixed with sin. It is in our very genetic makeup–all of us.

As we saw previously, in the New Testament, Paul makes it plain that there are two categories when it comes to our identities: flesh and Spirit.

The flesh belongs to the old realm. It is marred by sin.

The Spirit is God's own being working within us. He is in the process of renewing us and fitting us for Heaven.

When we make it to that kingdom, we will not experience, or be marred by, or be within an infinite number of miles of, any sinful, fleshly feelings.

Those will be gone. And that process starts now.

No one, then, can hang on to their homosexual identity and call it okay, neutral, sinless, or natural.

It is all still flesh. Even our very genes, again, are marred by sin.

We must ask God to renew us, all the time.

We cannot hang on to, coddle, or normalize any part of us that is contrary to the will of God, as unfair as it might feel—no inclination; no supposed identity; no desire.

But here is the caveat.

Some aspects of our identity *are* more fundamental than others. We should not deny this. And sexual orientation might not be, in the end, something that someone can completely control, change, alter, or improve.

In other words, some Christians might struggle with very instinctual temptations to this sin their whole lives.

I believe we have to allow room for such struggle.

God might change some people's sexual orientation, but often he does not fully do so. This is no different, really, than any other basic sinful impulse. I believe it can certainly be argued that we all have various instinctual desires, various orientations, if you will, that are in and of themselves sinful. We still must struggle against these, for all of life.

So too must the one who has same-sex attraction.

And I believe we must give that person room to struggle.

God always calls us to holiness.

But his mercy, patience, and long-suffering toward us are truly beyond our comprehension.

Once again, we must strive to keep these two perspectives in balance.

XIV.

Women in Church Leadership

THERE IS ANOTHER ISSUE causing confusion today; the issue of the role of women in church leadership.

Here I will be a bit more concise.

The New Testament is clear that women are not to be leaders in the church—that is, pastors or elders. Nor are they to teach men. It really is surprising how some attempt to explain the evidence away, as it is rather clear.

No doubt this is a such a difficult issue because of the spirit of our age. Equality for the sexes has long been the cry in our society.

Once again, I believe Christians should sympathize with this as much as they can.

It is good to recall the life of Jesus.

As is clear on every page of the gospel record, Jesus broke down all social barriers. He ministered to those of different races, different economic classes, and different social classes, including women and children, which in his day was unheard of.

He loved them, talked with them, and ministered to them.

To follow Jesus means to treat everyone with the same amount of respect that he showed them. As we have seen, it also means to treat those who have been abused, mistreated, neglected, and oppressed with special consideration, grace, and care.

In Jesus's day and for most of human history, women have been oppressed and abused by men.

This is why we must sympathize with this issue as much as we can.

We must seek avenues to allow for the ministry of women in the church. Furthermore, we must not, I believe, overly guard the speaking ministry of women. Not every speaking opportunity, perhaps, should be considered teaching or preaching.

Some have so guarded these things that they have made them central or major issues in the life of the church. Some have so guarded them that they literally have not allowed women to say a word in church, even in prayer.

Again, this should not be. Such churches, in my view, have not given full weight to the New Testament evidence regarding the role of women in early church life.

And yet, I want to reiterate; I do not believe there is any way to get around the New Testament's teaching on this issue. Paul makes it very clear that women are not to teach or exercise authority over men. He roots this command in the order of creation.

Some have argued that we can discard this command because many churches today have discarded Paul's command for women to cover their heads, and this command is also rooted in the creation order. So if we discard one, we can discard the other.

This will not suffice. The difference with head coverings is clear. Head coverings were a custom already in place before the church age, and they are obviously symbolic. Paul's command regarding head coverings seems to be that believers should continue this custom for the sake of order; he did not want it said that Christian women were discarding their roles.

Many theologians in modern times have argued that we need not continue to follow this ancient and largely symbolic cultural practice, though they may have argued this a bit too quickly.

Regardless, actual leadership in the church—that is, having authority over others—as well as teaching, are clearly not a matter of symbols. And these, Paul says, must be limited to men. This is God's design.

But this raises another facet of this discussion. Paul tells us on numerous occasions that in Christ, man and woman are equal, and that we should all submit to each other out of reverence for Jesus (Ephesians 5:21), our ultimate head.

I believe this also points to our future state in Heaven, when there will not be either marriage or the church. This should help us put this issue in proper balance.

There is some room for freedom here, I believe.

And yet—women are still not to teach or lead in the church.

The Word of God is clear, and we must strive to maintain biblical limits until the appointed time.

What then can women do in church?

Anything else that the Holy Spirit has truly gifted and called them to do.

God help the church to find those arenas, and to be careful not to exclude, ignore, or simply miss the God-given, Spirit-empowered ministries of all its members!

XV.

Truth and Unity

THERE IS A FINAL issue to be discussed; I believe this is an issue of great concern, and one that might present a real danger in the near future.

It also presents a real opportunity.

Great wisdom is needed.

The large "corporate" churches that we see today indicate that there may be a trend toward unity, at least among some groups.

Some of it is hopeful.

In several larger churches I have been in, great emphasis was put on the Great Commission, as I have said. But everything else was streamlined. Prayer was missing; statements of faith were trimmed; truth was often sacrificed for the sake of the gospel.

I believe Christians must be incredibly careful here.

We have already discussed how key truths from the Bible have disappeared in our day.

The disunity and division in the Christian church at large, especially the racial division, is a great tragedy. It surely grieves our Lord Jesus, who prayed for unity in his church.

Yet we cannot abandon truth for the sake of unity.

There is a flip side, of course. I grew up in a denomination that had a statement of faith so long that few people even knew what was in it or had carefully thought about it.

They hedged their circles of fellowship so closely that one couldn't help but feel it was inappropriate. These churches were small and eventually divided further among themselves. They were eventually passed by in the purposes of God. Today this denomination is an afterthought.

So we can go too far with truth.

But is this really the problem today, that we have too much doctrine?

Far from it, as we have already seen.

Unity, again, cannot come at the expense of truth.

When Jesus called his disciples to be one, he wanted them unified around himself, his father, and his teaching. In his great prayer on unity in John 17, our Lord's first request is that his people be made holy in the truth, which is his Word. He mentions the Word of God over and over; then he gets to unity.

Let me state it as clearly as I can: there is no real Christian unity without the truth of the Word of God.

Again, I am not arguing for long and complex statements of faith. I am arguing for essential truths, many of which have long been lost. And this, perhaps, is the crux of the matter; what used to be essential truths are now considered optional or unimportant in many churches.

Like the key parts of the gospel that are now missing in our churches, those we have discussed.

Like an emphasis on holiness or prayer.

Like a proper method for ministry.

Like full consideration of God's sovereignty.

Like the careful application of the entire Word of God–all of which is obviously intended by God for his people.

It is indeed mysterious to me that we can treat certain parts of the Word of God as optional.

There are some issues, to be sure, that are not entirely clear in the New Testament. Regarding these issues, of course, there might be genuine disagreement; and any disagreement over unclear issues should not cause division.

But this is not the problem in our day.

The problem, I would argue, is that many churches are abandoning or ignoring certain truths that are clear in the Word of God. In many cases, they are doing so in the name of church growth.

But there can be no real church growth without the preaching of the whole purpose of God (Acts 20:27).

Church leaders in our day are "shrinking" from this calling.

And so I say that in our day and age, when the trend in the church is toward pleasing men and superficiality of life and thinking, most Evangelical churches need a return to the truth.

Then we can begin to rebuild our unity.

Fellowship and community are essential. Small groups are helpful. But without the truth they are of little use.

There is such a thing, after all, as counterfeit Christian fellowship.

Working with other believers, even those in other Protestant denominations, is admirable. But one cannot forsake the truth to do so.

Again, the Holy Spirit and the Word of God have a unique relationship. You cannot have one without the other. Thus, no true unity, born of the Spirit, can exist without truth.

It all goes back to Jesus.

We cannot have Him–the true and living Word–or his Spirit without having *all* of him. All that he said and taught. All that he called us to do and be.

Only there, where Jesus is—the real, full, and complete Jesus—can genuine community be found.

We must get back to Jesus first. That has been the main point of this book.

Then all else will follow.

Conclusion

LET'S DISCUSS THE WAY forward.

The situation, I truly believe, is dire, whether we are willing to admit it or not.

But it is not hopeless.

First, we must get rid of known sin in our lives, at whatever cost.

Bitterness, unresolved conflicts or settled attitudes, immoral thoughts or behavior, excessive entertainments or pleasures, covetousness, greed, and all idols.

We must repent. We must make sacrifices. We must cut off right hands and pluck out right eyes (Matthew 5:29–30). We must put sin to death by the power of the Spirit.

If we do not, we cannot be confident that we have the Holy Spirit within us–that we are truly God's children.

At the same time, we cannot get too discouraged. Many of us earnestly desire to do what is right; many of us are truly trying to follow Jesus.

To these, I say: remember, God is not looking for perfection. And let us not forget that we cannot earn our salvation. Jesus did that for us.

Neither will God let his true children go. What he has begun in us, he will perfect until the day of Christ Jesus (Philippians 1:6). Our minds can rest content in the work of Christ and in the loving faithfulness of our sovereign God. They truly can. All genuine Christians have felt the burden of their sin and guilt removed at the foot of the cross–forever. We cannot forget that.

And yet–the true Christian presses onward. He is not content with remaining sin or persistent uselessness. He knows that God's will for his life is holiness–and that it must be achieved. His aim is ever forward, ever onward.

May God come and help us be of this spirit.

Next, we must open the Word of God daily and let it speak to us–all of it to all of us.

Then we must carve out time for prayer.

Alone, with our spouses, with our families, with our small groups, with our churches.

Without a commitment to prayer, change will not happen.

It's as simple as that.

Fourth, we must begin to reorder our time toward the kingdom of Heaven. This means eliminating things that might not be sinful but might otherwise be distracting.

This means more time in prayer and true fellowship with other believers, so that we might minister to and encourage each other and support the purposes of God around the world.

Fifth, we must consider new ways in which we ourselves might serve Jesus in his mission.

Might we, after all, be called of the Holy Spirit to engage personally in missions? Have we ever considered it? There are a variety of ways to be involved; have we ever put ourselves on the line?

Do we even know who our missionaries are? Do we know who is serving around the world? Do we know the struggles they might be facing? Do we know the needs of particular places in the world? Are we truly considering the state of God's kingdom across the globe?

What about serving in my local community? There are needs all around; am I content merely to sit back and let others do the work, or I am getting involved as Jesus did?

Are our ideals hindering our usefulness? Are we thinking as Americans, making decisions based more on politics, or are we thinking as Christians?

These are the things we must be considering.

The great apathy that has taken over our society and the church is insidious.

I fear we have long been in that dreaded state of lukewarmness that Jesus warns so strongly against (Revelation 3:16).

Spirit of the living God, awaken us before it is too late.

Lord Jesus, if even in the reading of this little book, we have somewhat regained our sight—

Let us now follow you.